KEEPING THE
ANNIE DODGE WAUNEKA'S LIFE OF SERVICE TO THE NAVAJO
ROPE STRAIGHT

Carolyn Niethammer

Salina Bookshelf, Inc.
A NAVAJO LANGUAGE PUBLISHING COMPANY

Library of Congress Cataloging-in-Publication Data

Niethammer, Carolyn J.
  Keeping the rope straight : Annie Dodge Wauneka's life of service to the Navajo /
written by Carolyn Niethammer ; edited by Jessie Ruffenach.-- 1st ed.
    p. cm.
  ISBN 13: 978-1-893354-72-2
  ISBN 10: 1-893354-72-5
(hardcover : alk. paper) 1. Wauneka, Annie Dodge, 1918-1997--Juvenile literature.
2. Navajo women--Biography--Juvenile literature. 3. Navajo Indians--Biography--
Juvenile literature. 4. Navajo Indians--Politics and government--Juvenile literature.
5. Navajo Indians--Health and hygiene--Juvenile literature. I. Ruffenach, Jessie. II.
Title.
E99.N3W386 2006
979.1004'97260092--dc22

                              2005026761

                       Edited by Jessie Ruffenach
                     Designed by Bahe Whitethorne, Jr.

                  Printed in the United States of America

                       First Printing, First Edition
                 12 11 10 09 08 07 06 10 9 8 7 6 5 4 3 2 1

                         Salina Bookshelf, Inc.
                        Flagstaff, Arizona 86001
                        www.salinabookshelf.com

Cover design by Bahe Whitethorne, Jr. The upper portion of the cover shows Annie Wauneka as
a child (courtesy of the Provincial Archives, St. Michaels Mission, F736.50-87 R9142); the lower
portion of the cover shows sheep on their way home at sunset (courtesy of Navajo Gospel Mission).

for Martha
— Carolyn

In memory of Brian, Melissa, and Audrey
Three inspired people whose work lives on
— Salina Bookshelf

Table of Contents

List of Illustrations

A Teacher and Guide

*Words from Dr. Peterson Zah, former President
of the Navajo Nation, on Annie Wauneka*

I t was 6 a.m. when the knock sounded at my door. It was a cold, windy morning; the sun had barely risen, and I was still in bed. As I awkwardly made my way to the door, I thought to myself, *"Hái lá t'ah t'áá 'abínígo shaa níyá?* Who could *possibly* be coming to see me so early?" The previous afternoon I had arranged to meet with Annie Dodge Wauneka, so we could discuss my campaign strategy; however, I didn't expect to see her until ten o'clock – eight o'clock at the earliest. It couldn't be her.

But I was wrong. When I opened the door, Annie Dodge Wauneka stood before me: tall, traditionally dressed, ready for a full day's work. She looked me up and down, no doubt carefully noting my wrinkled t-shirt and tousled hair. Then she said to me: *"Shą hxanii 'abínígo nídiishyeed dinii ne'.* I thought you said you were going to run. If you're going to run, you've got to get up early! We can't have a Tribal Chairman who gets up after the sun comes up!"

That was my first experience with Annie as my campaign advisor. She was very direct, very specific. I was learning immediately, and I was to benefit much more from her words as the morning wore on.

"*Shiyáázh*," she began, after I had gotten some coffee ready, "if you run for Tribal Chairman, you will have to visit each of the 80 chapters three times. On the first visit, just let people know who you are. Answer the question, 'Who is Pete Zah?' Tell the people that you live in Low Mountain, and that you have three children. Tell them that you have sheep, that you have a corral, and that you live in a hogan. Tell them that you know how to plant corn and that you *did* plant corn, squash, melons … tell the people that you know how to raise all these things, and that you went out in the morning and hoed the fields."

She smiled and poured herself more coffee. "And that's it! Then the second time you go out there, you can begin talking about your goals and aspirations, and what direction you think the Navajo people should be headed. On the third visit, come out with a specific program. Tell people your campaign platform."

Before she left that morning, she said, "I understand you're going to go out towards Eastern Navajo Agency on Thursday. *Akǫ́ǫ́ nił deesh'ash.* I'll go with you."

Thursday morning, I was ready for Annie when she knocked on my door. We drove out to the Eastern Navajo Agency, and I campaigned as Annie had instructed me: I introduced myself to the people and said nothing about economic development, education, or other issues. I thought the day went well, but as we drove back home, Annie gave me further advice.

"*Shiyáázh*, I watched you. People came up to you to shake your hand. But there were so many people who wanted to meet you that when you shook hands you didn't look the person in the eye. As you shook one person's hand, your eyes were moving on to the next person." She paused. "People don't appreciate that kind of treatment. When people come up to shake your hand, you have to recognize them individually. Look each person in the eye and thank them for coming in."

When I became *Diné 'aláají' yá dah sidáhígíí*, Tribal

Chairman[1], I deliberately left a space open for Annie. Her experience in politics and her knowledge of the many issues we were facing made her an invaluable advisor.

Annie loved to work. She loved the Navajo people. And she loved the land. "Look at these hills, these mesas," she would say. "Look at these beautiful juniper trees ... look at the terrain, the sky ... the rain and the snow. *Kéyah t'áánáwhíiz'áánít'ę́ę́' néél'íi'go. Ts'ídá aláahgo áhxoozhónígi kééwhiit'į.* We live in the most beautiful place on earth."

Annie never looked to get away from the Navajo Nation. She wanted to be where she was needed most, and she knew that place was with her own people. Dedicated 100 percent to the health, education, and welfare of the Navajo people, Annie worked tirelessly on every project she began. When she saw that something needed to be done, she would work to get it done, no matter how many obstacles stood in her way.

Her fight against the tuberculosis epidemic is a perfect example of her determination. When she became the chairperson of the Health and Welfare Committee, the first thing she did was to educate herself about tuberculosis. She made it her duty to learn everything she could about the disease. She said, "I want to *meet* tuberculosis. I want to find out what it is that's killing the Navajo people, and I want to find out *why*."

At every stage in the fight against tuberculosis, there were problems. But Annie surmounted them. In the beginning, there were no roads. So she drove out to the remote hogans in her truck. Next, there was no way for her to communicate her knowledge to the Navajo people. So she started her own radio program. Finally, sanatoriums needed to be built for all the sick people, but there was no money. So she went to Congress and got the money.

Nowadays, it is difficult to imagine someone facing all the

obstacles that Annie was confronted with as a politician. But Annie just kept on going. She knew what she needed to do, and giving up was something she never even considered.

In 1984, during my term as Tribal Chairman, the Navajo Nation held a special "Annie Wauneka Day" to honor Annie for her lifetime of service to the Navajo people. The event coincided with her 74th birthday, and during a ceremony she was awarded the Navajo Medal of Honor. The people in attendance came from many different places, often from great distances, in order to show their support and appreciation for all of Annie's work.

At the end of the day, Annie came to me. "*Shiyáázh*," she said, placing her hand on my arm, "this is worth more to me than all the other awards I have received."

To be so honored by her own people was the highest praise, the highest recognition she looked for.

[1] President

A Lasting Debt

*Words from Senator Albert Hale, former President
of the Navajo Nation, on Annie Wauneka*

When I was a child, I contracted tuberculosis. I was sick and my family knew I was sick, but, as I was part of a very traditional Navajo family, I was not taken to a hospital. One Navajo traditional practice is to avoid contact with dead people and everything associated with them, for it is believed that being near death will contaminate you. When I was young, that tradition extended to the hospitals. People died in hospitals, and my family, like many other families, refused to go to a hospital even if they were extremely ill.

My family called in many medicine men to perform ceremonies, but I grew weaker with every passing day. One evening, as my mother held me, she realized that something else needed to be attempted. We didn't have any vehicles, but she walked down to a trading post, which was about a mile away. She found someone with a truck, brought him back to the hogan, and persuaded him to drive me to the hospital. I remained at the hospital for two months, maybe even three months. I recovered.

My mother's decision to take me to a hospital was a difficult one for her to make. However, it was a decision she probably would never have made if it had not been for Annie Wauneka. Annie Wauneka had been going from hogan to hogan, educating people, telling families what to do if someone in the hogan became sick with tuberculosis. Annie always encouraged people to go to the hospital if they were ill.

That was the first time Annie Wauneka saved my life. But she saved my life again not many years later.

One fall, at the beginning of my junior year at Ganado High School, my brother Ronald and I were unable to begin school on time because we didn't have any suitable clothing. My family was poor, and my mother had to sell some sheep before we had enough money to buy clothes. At last, one week after the start of classes, my brother and I made it to school. However, the principal wouldn't let us begin late. "There's no way you'll be able to catch up," he told us. "Go back home."

We left the school. My brother, who was older than I was, later joined the military service. Before he did that, we went down to the Glendale, Arizona, area and worked as migrant farm workers. It was the hardest work I ever did, and during those long days out in the fields, I realized I needed to get back into school. I needed an education. However, I delayed; I was reluctant to go back to a place from which I had been turned away.

During this time, I often attended the Klagetoh chapter meetings at which Annie spoke. She was an eloquent speaker, and the skill with which she delivered her speeches held her listeners spellbound. When she spoke, everyone was focused, everyone was listening, everyone was looking at her. No one fidgeted, and no restless murmurs rose from the crowd. When discussing weighty issues, she would say, "*T'áadoo le'í mdazígíí baa jiláágo doo nidaaz da,*" which when translated means, "If there is something heavy, if you all work together, then it will be light." In other words, "If only one person tries to do it, it will be heavy." She was forever empowering people to confront and solve problems, saying, "*Bił dashdoolnih,*" or "(with support) you can do it."

At one of the chapter meetings, Annie, much to my surprise, stood up and began addressing me directly. "Albert Hale," she said, shaking her finger at me, "what are you doing here?" As I sank lower and lower in my chair, she continued: "I want you to go back to school. I want you to finish school, and I want you to make something of yourself. I don't want you hanging around here just becoming a local drunk."

Annie had a talent for admonishing people in a way that wasn't critical of the person. She criticized what you were doing, not you as a person, and she spoke in such a way that made you really think about what you were doing. After the meeting, I asked myself, "What *am* I doing?" I went back to school. I graduated. I went to college and then to law school. It is easy to settle into a routine and make the best of it; however, sometimes we need others to come up behind us and prod us to do more. We need someone to tell us, "*Bił dashdoolnih.*"

Annie was that person for me, as she was for many others privileged enough to be acquainted with her. Annie knew, perhaps more than any other person I've ever met, that one person can make a difference in the world. That difference might be small and seemingly insignificant, but still it is something. Annie saw that potential in me, just as she saw it in herself.

It is unusual to be indebted to someone for saving your life even once. Annie Wauneka saved mine at least twice.

Keeping The Rope Straight

Map of the Navajo Nation

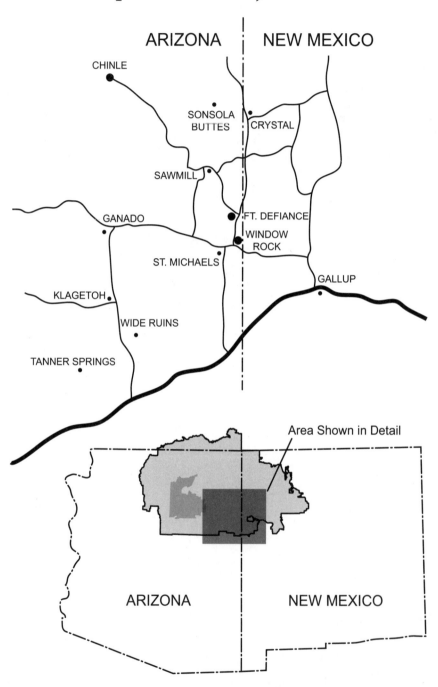

ARIZONA | NEW MEXICO

CHINLE

SONSOLA
BUTTES
CRYSTAL

SAWMILL

GANADO
FT. DEFIANCE
WINDOW
ROCK

ST. MICHAELS

GALLUP

KLAGETOH

WIDE RUINS

TANNER SPRINGS

Area Shown in Detail

ARIZONA | NEW MEXICO

Introduction

For 26 years, Annie Dodge Wauneka served her people on the Navajo Tribal Council. She worked to help educate Navajos about tuberculosis, a disease that was infecting thousands of Navajos. She also cooperated with doctors and nurses to bring better nutrition and child care to Navajo families, and she was always interested in education. She traveled to Washington, DC, more than twenty times to speak to the Senate and House of Representatives on behalf of the Navajos. But Annie started her life like most children of her day, as a sheepherder.

Annie Wauneka.
(Courtesy National Archives, photo no. 220-IWB-5-11.)

Chapter 1

It was still dark when five-year-old Annie was awakened by the stirring of the household. It was cold, but she knew there would be a warm fire in the kitchen. She quickly got up and put on her shoes, then brushed her long, dark hair and tied it with a string.

In the kitchen, a fire blazed in the big, black cookstove and water boiled in a blue enamel coffeepot. Annie poured herself a glass of water from a pitcher on the table. Although it was cozy next to the stove, she knew she couldn't linger. She put on her jacket, tied a head scarf under her chin, and made her way out to the sheep corral. As soon as she stepped out the door, her dog ran up to her, excited to know that they would be heading away from the ranch. The sun had just come up over the Chuska mountains, turning the cliffs golden.

As she neared the sheep pens, her dog at her heels, Annie could smell the mixture of dust and manure. The animals were bleating and snuffling as they milled about, ready to be released. Three strong herders, men who worked for Annie's father, Chee Dodge, had already drawn water for the sheep. The men were busy separating the sheep into flocks that they would be leading to pasture for the day.

Annie let herself into the corral and found the sheep that she would be taking. She recognized her own animals, ones her father had given her, by their ear marks, and she also took some that her mother and father expected her to watch for them. She led the sheep about a half mile from the house to a grassy area, laughing at the antics of the smallest lambs as they ran alongside their mothers. When Annie found a spot with tall grass, she first checked to see if there were any weeds that would make the sheep sick. After determining that all the plants were safe, she found a flat rock and sat down to watch the sheep begin to graze. When she was sure that the sheep were settled, she commanded her dog to watch over them and trudged back to her house for a quick breakfast.

Unlike most Navajos of the early 1900s, Annie did not live in a hogan. Her father was Chee Dodge, a wealthy rancher and a Navajo leader. He had hired an architect from Flagstaff (*Kin Łání Dook'o'oosłííd Biyaagi*, "many houses below San Francisco Peaks"), Arizona, to design a house of four large rooms with a big porch across the whole front. The house was built on a slight slope, so people coming in the front climbed up wooden stairs to the porch and front door. Many relatives were always coming and going from the Dodge home, some staying for months to work as herders or to do other chores. Some low buildings behind the main house provided rooms and sleeping space for workers and visiting relatives.

Because Chee Dodge was one of the five appointed head men of the Navajo tribe and was one of the very few Navajos who spoke English well, officials from the United States government were occasional visitors. Navajos who wanted to discuss reservation politics or issues with the federal or state government frequently stopped by to get Chee Dodge's views or advice.

In the kitchen of the big house, Annie's mother, Nanabah, and her aunt, Asza Yaze, both of whom were married to Chee,

Home of Henry Chee Dodge near Crystal, New Mexico.
(Courtesy of the Navajo Nation Museum, Window Rock, AZ, Catalog No. NAV-176.)

bustled about. They patted dough into big, flat rounds and eased it into a pan of hot fat. It was not unusual at that time for Navajo sisters or cousins to be married to the same man. There was a great deal of work to be done in a large household like Chee's, and the two sisters were able to share the labor. Most Navajo homes were built far away from each other, and having a sister or cousin nearby meant that the women had some companionship in a lonely area.

In Chee's household, Nanabah and Asza Yaze shared the childrearing, household management, and cooking. When the fry bread was golden on one side, whoever was cooking that day used a long-handled fork to turn it and brown the other side. The smell was delicious, and even though Annie had the same breakfast every day, her mouth watered as she awaited her piece. Annie ate her fry bread with a cup of weak coffee. Today, coffee is not considered a healthy drink for children, but in those days, all Navajos drank weak coffee.

As soon as Annie had finished her breakfast, she took another piece of fry bread and a bottle of water, wrapped them in a cloth for her lunch, and went back to the sheep. She stayed with the sheep for the rest of the day, moving them along when they had eaten all the grass in a particular spot. It wasn't until late in the afternoon, when the sun was getting low in the sky, that Annie and her dog began to urge the sheep back home, where they were locked safely in the corral for the night.

The days were rather lonely for such a young child, but Annie was no ordinary little girl. From a young age, she was very strong and independent. She made her own toys and games. Years later, she told a friend how she had invented a game for herself to help pass the time. She gathered many small, white stones and these were the sheep she watched over. There was also a black stone representing the dangerous coyote, which was looking for a tasty meal of lamb. We can imagine that it was Annie herself who was

Sheep on their way home at sunset.
(Courtesy of Navajo Gospel Mission.)

the rescuer of those poor sheep, keeping them safe. In another game, she set up ant battles. She brought black ants to anthills built by red ants and amused herself by watching how the red ants reacted to the invaders.

Annie's father, Chee Dodge, could have easily hired herders to watch over all the sheep, but he thought it would be good for Annie to learn about hard work. Annie had two older brothers, Tom and Ben, and an older sister Mary. These children were sent off the reservation to private Catholic schools. It was never quite clear why Chee decided that only Annie, his youngest child, should spend so much time herding sheep.

Eventually, however, in the fall of 1918, Chee decided that it was time Annie learned English and how to read. When she was eight, he allowed her to go to the government school at Fort Defiance (*Tséhootsooí*, "meadow in between the rocks"). Today it is a short car ride from Fort Defiance to Chee's ranch at Sonsola Buttes (*Sǫ Sílá*, "stars lying down"), but in those days, the horseback or wagon trip took many hours. As a result, Annie boarded at the school.

In the early years when the United States government was just beginning to get involved in Navajo affairs, Chee understood the importance of education for his people. Because he had been an orphan and had to work to support himself at a young age, he had only received a few months of schooling. But Chee always supported education and sent his children to school as an example to other Navajos.

Annie loved school and learning, but within a few short months after her arrival, her studies had to stop. What happened over the next few months would influence the path her life would take as an adult, but she did not know this at the time.

A terrible epidemic of Spanish influenza was sweeping over the entire planet and it did not spare the Navajo Reservation. As this was during World War I, the flu spread rapidly. American troops were traveling to Europe and back, bringing the flu with them. This strain of flu was highly contagious, spreading through coughs and sneezes.

Chee sent for his older children Tom, Ben, and Mary to come home from their schools. Once they were safely home, he locked the gate into his ranch to prevent anyone from entering and infecting his family with the terrible virus. For reasons we will never know, he did not call Annie home.

The flu was introduced to the Fort Defiance school by a sick Navajo man who had been visiting in Zuni. He contracted the virus there, and then came to the school to work. Ten days later, 250 students and 20 of the teachers and other staff were ill. Annie herself got a mild case of the flu. Fortunately, probably because of her strong constitution, she recovered. Soon the school was quarantined as more of the residents became ill.

Looking back on that time, Annie recalled, "I remember that little wooden hospital. There were lots and lots of sick students, there were hundreds of students. These students were full grown adults, men and boys, big fellows that went to school. At first one or two died, pretty soon they were just dying like flies."

After all the other teachers and helpers got ill, there was only one nurse to watch over everyone, Mrs. Domatilda Showalter. With Annie as her only assistant, Mrs. Showalter attempted to care for everyone. Electricity had not reached Fort Defiance yet, so every day Annie had to clean and fill the kerosene lanterns. Annie remembered Mrs. Showalter saying, "Would you wash these lanterns and make them bright and shiny?" Annie saw the other students come into the hospital by the dozens. Every bed was full. She spoon-fed soup to the people who were too weak to feed themselves.

But the students arriving at the hospital stayed only a day or two. The flu virus filled their lungs with blood, they became unable to breathe, and soon died. At first, each student was put into a coffin, but soon there was no one left to build more coffins or to help with the burials.

Annie remembered, "They'd just wrap them up in a sheet and pile them on top of each other, just pile them. Five or ten were dying every night. There were horse-driven wagons and they used to just pile up the bodies like a bunch of wood and haul them away."

The Spanish flu was unusual in the way it attacked its victims. Usually flu affects very young children or older people who are already weakened. But the Spanish flu took the young and strong. On the Navajo Reservation, as many as 2,500 people died. The fact that Navajos tend to live far away from each other probably prevented more of them from getting sick.

Today it is very difficult for us to read about this period of time, and we can only imagine how frightening it must have been for eight-year-old Annie, who was away from home for the first time in her life.

When spring came, the school was closed and those students who had survived went back to their homes. Chee sent a wagon for Annie to take her back to Sonsola Buttes. When she got back to the ranch, she was surprised to see her brothers and sister already back from private school. This surprise caused her to start wondering why she was being treated differently from the other children in her family.

During the summer Annie slipped back into her former routine of taking the sheep out in the morning and bringing them back in the evening.

A well-trained sheep herd will stay bunched together, but occasionally any group of sheep may decide to scatter. These nimble-footed animals can scamper up a rocky hillside very quickly, leaving their human minders far behind. One bluff near the range where Annie took her sheep was particularly attractive

St. Michaels Indian School.
(Courtesy of the Provincial Archives, St. Michaels Mission, S146b9-41 R10555.)

to the animals. After Annie spent one too many times having to take a long trail to the top of the bluff to collect her sheep, she finally installed a rope that would help her climb up the cliff. Many years later, when she was an old woman taking a drive by the area with her daughter, she wondered if that rope were still there.

In the fall, Annie was allowed to go back to school in Fort Defiance. However, when spring arrived and the pregnant sheep began to deliver their lambs, she was expected to come back to the ranch to help, whether the school session was over or not.

When Annie was in the fourth grade, sickness struck her school again. This time it was trachoma, a very infectious disease of the eyelids. It is very uncomfortable because it feels like tiny grains of sand are in your eye. The children would rub their eyes, then touch each other or a towel, or even share a pencil, every time passing the virus to their fellow students. Trachoma is not only uncomfortable, but also dangerous. If it is not treated, trachoma can lead to blindness.

All the children who were not yet infected were transferred to St. Michaels Catholic Mission school about 10 miles away. During this time, while Annie was being taught by the nuns at St. Michaels (*Ts'íhootso*, "yellow meadow"), she received her first religious instruction. We can't be sure how much choice the children had in the matter, but Annie was baptized and confirmed in the Catholic church. She was to attend mass regularly for the rest of her life, frequently attending the mission church at St. Michaels.

The trachoma epidemic raged for about a year and a half, and when it was finally brought under control, Annie returned to school at Fort Defiance. Annie's sister Mary was not happy being away at school in Denver, so her father let her come home and attend school in Fort Defiance also.

Mary and Annie never got along well, and now that Mary was

Five Indian girls. Annie is second from the right.
(Courtesy of the Provincial Archives, St. Michaels Mission, F736.50-87 R9142.)

home and she and Annie were attending the same school, they were together more. Sometimes Mary would tease her saying, "You don't belong with us, you're from another family."

Then Annie would go to Nanabah and ask, "Are you my mother?" When Nanabah said she was, Annie would counter with, "Well, Mary said...."

"Don't listen to her," Nanabah would tell Annie. "Mary is just being a troublemaker."

When Annie had finished the fifth grade, the Albuquerque Indian School was opened to all Indian students. Because Annie had been doing so well in school, Chee decided to send both Annie and Mary there, thinking they might receive a better education than at Fort Defiance.

The children, along with the trunks, were loaded on a horse-drawn wagon early one morning before the sun had even peeked over Sonsola Buttes. We can imagine the girls were excited to be going to the new school. The wagon took them to the railroad station in Gallup (*Na'nízhoozhí*, "spanned across"), New Mexico. Mary was told to look after her little sister Annie until they were safely at school. Other Navajo children had come with their parents, and the mood was very festive as they all boarded a train headed for Albuquerque (*Bee'eldííldahsinil*, "at the place of the (bell) peals"), New Mexico.

As the train made its way east, Annie was interested in watching the countryside pass by. When lunchtime came, she and Mary ate the lunch Nanabah had packed for them. In the evening, when they had not much farther to travel, the train stopped at Laguna Pueblo (*Tó Łání*, "much water") to pick up some local children. As the new children were boarding with their luggage, a great commotion began. The few adults who were supervising the children began running through the cars, urging the youngsters to run to the front of the train. Another train was about to crash into their train from the rear. The situation was made worse by the fact that many of the children did not understand English and did not know what to do; nevertheless, they did start to run.

As Annie told the story, "I was running too and heard this great big locomotive – the head just plowed into the back of our train, derailed some of it, and all of us just fell on top of each other. Some of the students jumped from the windows and broke their hips and their arms. We just fell on top of each other in this big train."

The grown-ups finally got all the children off the train and began to tend to those who were injured. They told those children who were not hurt to sit under a big tree until they decided where they would go next. Mary told Annie to watch the luggage and went off to explore with some older girls. Annie, who knew no one, sat guarding the luggage. No one came to tell her what to do. Other older children also wandered off. Soon the night grew dark and chilly. The moon rose and still she sat alone, with no supper and nothing to drink. It was a very frightening night for her. At last, morning came and the wrecked train was cleared away. Another train was sent for the children, and later that day, they arrived at their new school.

Annie was very happy at Albuquerque Indian School. She made friends quickly, particularly with girls from some of the New Mexico pueblos. Although she never knew her grandmother, Annie knew that her father's mother had been part Jemez Pueblo, so she felt a kinship with these girls.

The Albuquerque school also offered music and sports and Annie learned to play tennis and appreciate classical music. Mary, on the other hand, was not happy at the Albuquerque school and convinced her parents to let her come home. Back at Sonsola Buttes, Mary worked handing out supplies to the people who worked for her father.

In 1922, when Annie was attending school in Albuquerque, the United States government decided that the Navajos needed a governing body to speak for them in legal matters. The Navajos did not traditionally have a chief like some other tribes, so the government appointed a business council. Since many of the officials in Washington, DC, already knew Chee Dodge, he was one of the three men appointed to the new council. Later the officials decided there needed to be a tribal council of elected delegates, and Chee became the first elected chairman of the Navajo tribe. In his new role, Chee, along with some of the other delegates, visited Albuquerque Indian School and spoke to the students in an assembly, urging them to study hard to prepare to lead the Navajos into modern life.

Annie was in the audience, and how proud she was to see her handsome father on the stage in front of all the other students!

Annie had begun to learn English at school in Fort Defiance and St. Michaels because the Navajo children were forbidden to speak their own language in school. This was true at the Albuquerque Indian School as well. Annie recalled, "I and many of my Pueblo friends decided that we were going to speak the very best English that we could."

This hard work led to very good report cards for Annie – mostly *A*'s with just a few *B*'s. She advanced quickly, covering two grades each year, making up for the years she had missed. Now Annie was allowed to stay in school all year, coming home only for summer vacation.

During the summers, Annie would sometimes visit her aunt Keehanabah in Sawmill (*Ni'iijíhi*, "sawery"), Arizona, and play with Keehanabah's children. Kehanabah, who was a half-sister of Nanabah, lived in a traditional hogan. Living in a hogan was a big change for Annie, who was accustomed to living in a house.

Henry Chee Dodge boards the train in Gallup, New Mexico, to leave for Washington, DC. Photo taken May 10, 1954.
(Photographed by Milton Snow, Courtesy of the Navajo Nation Museum, Window Rock, AZ, Catalog No. NO9-87.)

Sometimes Keehanabah would buy some lengths of fabric, and Annie would help her sew it into clothing for the smaller children.

But these summer breaks were hardly vacations for Annie. "Every time I went home during the summer vacation, all I did was sheepherding," she recalled. "Every time I'd come home, there'd be a batch of sheep sittin'. The next morning I had to get going."

Annie always looked forward to going back to school in Albuquerque in the fall. But toward the end of her junior year in high school, she learned that her happy life as a scholar would soon end.

Chapter 2

Because Annie was completing two grades each year, she had caught up with and moved ahead of others her age. One fall, upon returning to school, she found herself in a class with a good-looking young Navajo boy named George Wauneka. George, who had grown up in Blue Canyon (*Bikooh Hodootłizh*, "blue canyon"), near Fort Defiance, was several years older than Annie. He was on the school football team.

It was a wonderful year for Annie at school, but it was to be her last. Chee's new duties as tribal chairman frequently kept him away from Sonsola Buttes. He was often traveling to various parts of the reservation, gathering information and informing the Navajos of new events. So when Annie finished eleventh grade, Nanabah told her that she needed to stay home to help with the sheep. She would not be going back to school. By this time, the household's herds of sheep, goats, and cattle numbered in the thousands. Once again, Annie's life, so rich while at school, settled into the old routine of taking the sheep out in the morning, watching over them all day, and bringing them back in the late afternoon.

Annie also had lessons in how to be a good Navajo housewife. She learned how to sew, how to cook stews and make tortillas, how to butcher so that all parts of the animal could be used, and how to process the wool from the sheep and weave rugs. Although both Nanabah and Asza Yaze wove beautiful rugs, Annie never became interested in rug weaving.

Around this time, Annie's sister Mary married a boy named Carl Peshlaki. They lived at Sonsola Buttes for a while, but Chee had other plans for them. He had purchased another ranch he called Tanner Springs (*K'ai' Si'ání,* "sitting willow") south of Ganado (*Lók'aahnteel,* "wide band of reeds up at an elevation") by Wide Ruins (*Kinteel,* "wide house"). He kept his cattle at Tanner Springs, and sent some of his sheep there for the winter. It was a little warmer there and safer for the animals. He decided that Mary and Carl should watch over his affairs at Tanner Springs.

At some point after Mary left, Annie told her father about George Wauneka, the boy she had met at Albuquerque Indian School. There were no clan taboos to prevent them from marrying, so Chee and Nanabah approved the match.

George and Annie were married in a traditional Navajo wedding ceremony at the Tanner Springs ranch in October 1929. The young couple sat on the west side of a brush shelter with a small pot of water with a gourd ladle and a basket filled with *txaadniil,* unflavored corn mush, in front of them. A medicine man conducted the ceremony and gave the blessing. Many of the guests rode in on horseback or came in wagons, some from a great distance, because Chee was so well-known on the reservation.

Annie wore a printed tiered cotton skirt and a long-sleeved velvet blouse for her wedding. Her long, black hair was pulled back tightly and tied with white yarn in a *tsiiyéél* or double bun. Chee had lent her many pieces of his large collection of silver and turquoise jewelry – strings of turquoise beads, several bracelets, and rings. She wore a Pendleton blanket over her shoulders.

Annie and George exchanging wedding vows with a traditional Navajo medicine man.
(Courtesy of the Navajo Nation Museum, Window Rock, AZ, Catalog No. NAV-228.)

George Wauneka, Henry Chee Dodge, and Annie Wauneka.
(Photographed by Milton Snow, Courtesy of the Navajo Nation Museum, Window Rock, AZ, Catalog No. NO9-265.)

George wore a red scarf around his forehead and some necklaces. After the wedding, all the guests stayed for a big feast of *dibé yázhí sit'éego* or barbecued lamb, tortillas, beans, and other delicious food. Annie's mother, Nanabah, was not present at the wedding. According to the older Navajo ways, a mother-in-law avoids her daughter's husband.

After the wedding, Annie and George went to live at Sonsola Buttes and work for Chee. They were industrious and received no special favors from the old man; he treated them just like his other hired help. George was a pleasant, easy-going fellow, and Chee came to like and trust him so much that he put George in charge of all his sheep. But down at Tanner Springs, Mary was unhappy to be so far from her mother. Chee decided to bring her and Carl back to the main ranch and send Annie and George to Tanner Springs with its many hundreds of head of cattle. So, one day the young couple packed their belongings into a wagon and left for the remote ranch, taking their own herds of sheep with them.

Tanner Springs is at the end of a long dirt road, far removed from any neighbors. The home Annie and George lived in was just a simple wooden cabin. But the area is very beautiful. The south is bordered by La Pinta Mesa and the land slopes gently into the Painted Desert. It has less rain than the area around Sonsola Buttes and the storms usually come in the summer months.

Chee didn't just send Annie and George down to the ranch and leave them to figure out what to do. He gave them definite instructions about how he wanted them to operate the ranch. And he expected the young couple to carry out his orders to the letter. "He comes around and leaves instructions for us," Annie recalled. "I want the cattle sale on this date, and I want the calves branded on this date. I'll be here on this day and I want the report from you."

Caring for livestock is a job that needs to be done every single day, no matter what the weather. In the summer the sun beats down, turning the day into an oven; and in the winter the wind blows needles of snow and ice into your face. Years later, Annie remembered one job in particular, caring for her father's bulls that were used to breed his prize cattle. The bulls were kept in a corral several miles from their cabin. Annie had to walk on a trail through the sagebrush in order to pump water for the bulls. The bulls were bad-tempered and sometimes charged if they were in a bad mood. It took a great deal of courage for Annie to lift the heavy wooden gate and enter their pen to fill the trough.

There were usually a few other herders working for Chee and caring for some of the sheep. Whenever they were in the main camp, it was Annie's job to cook for them. She made big pots of stew, chile, and beans. These she served with flour tortillas. One frequent visitor remembers that Annie would pull up her skirt and roll the tortillas out on her leg before baking them on the griddle. Whenever anyone left the ranch, she sent them off with a big stack of delicious, fresh tortillas.

Annie had learned to be a hard worker when she was a child, so she was not used to an easy life. She also tried to work hard to please her handsome, famous father and win his approval. She knew that she had been treated differently than his older children, and she was striving to find a place in his affection.

As a child, Annie knew more about tribal politics than most youngsters her age because her father had been involved in the tribe's affairs for years. There were always visitors at the house at Sonsola Buttes and debates that went long into the night. Now that she was an adult, Chee thought it was time for Annie and George to learn more about the workings of the tribe. Sometimes after Chee had stopped at the Tanner Springs ranch to check on his affairs, he would take George and Annie to a chapter meeting at Wide Ruins or Klagetoh (*Łeeyi'tó*, "water in the ground").

Chapters are like counties in state governments, with elected officials who handle local issues. These chapter meetings were held under a big tree because a chapter house had not been built yet.

Many Navajos knew Chee Dodge, and those who didn't would come to a gathering he was attending just to meet him. It was like a president or a governor coming to visit, but even more than that. Chee was the richest and most successful Navajo rancher, and when he spoke, people could tell that he cared deeply about what happened to his fellow Navajos. He talked to them about how to improve their livestock by better breeding, how to care for the land, and advised them to send their children to school.

Sometimes there would be an important issue that Chee wanted to discuss with his neighbors. He would send Annie's husband George out on horseback to announce that a meeting would be held at the ranch on a particular day. Although Navajo women had a lot to say in how things were run in their own households, it was always men who came to the meetings. On the appointed day, Annie's house would fill with men wearing their big, flat, black hats. Among them were medicine men and the most important ranchers from the area. Chee ordered Annie to have plenty of mutton stew and coffee ready for the guests. Frequently, the men would stay up and talk all night. Despite the fact that Annie would have all her usual ranch chores to do the next day, Chee expected Annie to stay up, too, to keep the food ready.

But Annie wasn't content to just stay in the kitchen and cook and clean up. She had the benefit of a good education, both in school and at home, and she was interested in what was going on. That wasn't what Chee expected.

Annie recalled, "After I'm through with my dishes, I would come in and sit in the corner and he would say, 'What do you want to do here?'

"And I'd say, 'I want to listen to what you are going to talk about.'

"'You'd better boil some coffee,' he'd say.

"'I have it on the stove.'"

In this way, Annie continued her political education. It was a time of stress and change for the Navajos. Modern ways were overcoming important traditions. But the most important issue that was affecting everyone was the need to reduce the number of sheep, horses, and cattle on the reservation. The 1930s were a period of low rainfall on the reservation, and in many places grass was sparse. To have good range management, herders should be able to move their livestock to new pastures once the grass is eaten down. Then they don't bring their animals back to that spot until the grass has had time to recover. But with 1,300,000 sheep and goats on the reservation, there were not enough grassy areas to move them around. When the land has too much grass eaten, we say it is "over-grazed." Land that is over-grazed for too long never recovers and becomes dusty and barren. At that time there weren't a great many cattle on the reservation, but some Navajos had small herds. Horses added to the problem, with their numbers reaching 75,000. This was many more horses than were needed for transportation.

United States government officials decided that the Navajos would have to reduce the number of animals on the range and told Navajo leaders to help figure out a way to do that fairly. This was not easy, for at that time all of Navajo life was centered on their flocks of sheep. A family's wealth and place in society depended on how many sheep they owned. A family with many sheep was considered hard working, an important trait among Navajos. And sheep were very important in religion. When people traveled a great distance to attend a traditional ceremony, they had to be fed and they expected plenty of mutton. Horses also were very

Navajo Council Delegates listening to Albert Sandoval, who is interpreting for BIA Superintendent Stewart. Henry Chee Dodge and Sam Ahkeah, Navajo Vice-Chairman, are seated with Stewart at the front of the room.

(Photographed by Milton Snow, Courtesy of the Navajo Nation Museum, Window Rock, AZ, Catalog No. NO11-351.)

important to show how wealthy a family was. A white family might show how much money they had by having a large house with many rooms; wealthy Navajos might live in a small hogan, but have many horses.

Chee and the other Navajo leaders talked about ways that the number of animals might be reduced, but they could not come to an agreement. Finally, the government sent experts in range management. They traveled all over the reservation, looking at the condition of the land, and they were very worried by what they saw. The land was already in trouble and was wearing away due to erosion. The range management experts decided the number of animals needed to be reduced to just one-fifth of the current number.

Meetings were scheduled in every corner of the reservation, calling the people to hear the difficult news. Annie attended one of these meetings at the Klagetoh chapter. A government agent was discussing in English how each family would be required to get rid of more than half of their sheep. Because the people listening to him spoke only Navajo, a translator was trying to repeat the ideas in the Navajo language. Annie was shocked at how bad the translation was. Some of it was wrong and some of it was just plain confusing. Annie didn't speak up in the meeting. But that night when she went home, she mentioned it to her father, who happened to be at the Tanner Springs Ranch.

Chee Dodge exploded at his daughter. "And you just sat there and listened?" he demanded. "I sent you to school in Albuquerque to be educated so you could help your people, and you just sat there?"

"Boy, did I get the biggest scolding of my life," Annie said.

Chee's reaction was a great change from a few years earlier, when he had wanted Annie to stay in the kitchen to boil coffee and make mutton stew while he and the other men discussed events. It was also a major turning point in Annie's life. Many years after this event, whenever she gave a talk at meetings or in schools, she would tell that story.

During these years, Annie and George started their family. Their first child was Georgia Ann, born in 1931. They eventually had eight children, two girls and six boys. Their second child died shortly after birth.

So in addition to her ranch duties, Annie was giving attention to her children as well. Because the Tanner Springs ranch was so remote, Annie had to stock up on food for her family and the hired hands in case bad weather closed the road. She filled the underground storage room with 25-pound bags of flour, from which she would be able to make bread, tortillas, and fry bread. Big 100-pound sacks of beans and potatoes meant there would be plenty to eat even if the ranch were snowed in for weeks.

In those days the beans were not as clean as those we buy in plastic bags today. So with her children sitting around the table at night, Annie spread the beans out and taught the youngsters how to count as they picked through the beans to get rid of the little rocks, sticks, and leaves. When the beans were clean, Annie rinsed them and put them in a big pot on the back of the wood cookstove. They simmered slowly all night and were ready for breakfast the next morning.

Annie made other delicious Navajo dishes for her family. One of these was *dlǫ́ǫ́' sit'éego*, baked prairie dogs. When George caught four or five of the little animals, Annie would burn off the hair and clean the insides. Then she would stuff them with wild plants and herbs and close them up. She would bake them in the ground over coals until the meat was juicy and the skin was crisp.

Annie was also a very good butcher. When the family needed meat, she would choose one of the sheep to slaughter. The muscle parts of the sheep were roasted or cut up for stew. She made ch'iiyáán aláago nihxiłi kanígíí, a special Navajo dish, by

Henry Dodge Farm.
(Leslie Goodluck Collection, Cline Library, Northern Arizona University. Catalog No. NAU.PH.2003.13.4.2.)

catching the blood and mixing it with blue cornmeal, flour, fat, onions, potatoes, and tiny pieces of meat chopped from the neck bones. The mixture was then put in the cleaned sheep's stomach, tied up, and boiled until it was solid and had turned into a kind of sausage.

It was important to Annie to never waste any part of an animal she slaughtered. She always told her children, "If you just eat the muscle meat and throw away the rest of the sheep, you'll be the first to starve during a famine. Use every bit of the sheep, or you'll wish for the food you threw away." This is similar to the advice from mothers in other parts of the country who have told their children to eat their bread crusts or they will find themselves wanting them when food is scarce.

In 1939, when Annie was about 28 years old, Chee sent word to Tanner Springs that Nanabah had died. Annie rushed to Sonsola Buttes and was quite upset. When she got there and entered the big house, her father had some astounding news for her. What he had to tell her changed the way she looked at her entire family.

Chapter 3

Annie traveled to Sonsola Buttes by wagon and it took her some time to get there. When she finally arrived, Ben and Tom and Mary were there, along with many relatives. Annie was weeping at the loss of Nanabah, when Chee rather roughly chided her for her sorrow. "You shouldn't be crying so much," he said. "She wasn't even your mother."

For a moment, Annie was stunned, but then she began to piece together many memories from her childhood. At last, what she had long wondered about was found to be true.

Later, Chee told Annie the details of her birth. Keehanabah, the aunt she had visited so frequently in Sawmill, was actually her mother. Many years before, Nanabah and Asza Yaze, sisters and co-wives of Chee Dodge, had a disagreement with him and had left for home, taking their sheep with them. This was considered a Navajo divorce.

Because Chee was the most well-known and wealthiest man in the tribe, the family of the two women sent him another woman, a cousin of the other two, to act as his wife. Keehanabah was not happy in the big house at Sonsola Buttes, so when her cousins decided to come back to Chee, she was happy to return to her home in Sawmill. By that time she was pregnant, and Annie was born and lived her first eight months in Keehanabah's snug hogan. When the baby Annie was able to leave her mother, Chee and Nanabah picked her up and took her to the big house to grow up with her half-brothers Tom and Ben and half-sister Mary. Everyone managed to keep the secret until Nanabah's death, when Chee finally decided to tell Annie the truth.

The story of Annie's birth may have had something to do with the fact that Annie was treated less well than Chee's older children, but we do not know the details and why this made a difference to Chee.

As Annie continued her interest in Navajo tribal affairs, she began going to chapter meetings in Klagetoh either by herself or with her husband George. She became known as a clear thinker and speaker, and her neighbors elected her to the Grazing Committee. Members of the Grazing Committee tried to straighten out disagreements over who had rights to what pastures. They also set up times for people to bring their sheep and cattle in for vaccinations and to be dipped so they would avoid diseases. Later on, Annie was elected chapter secretary.

Annie had been rather shy as a child because she had spent so much time alone herding sheep, but as the years passed, she traveled with her father and learned from him as she watched him perform before crowds. Holding chapter office also gave her confidence.

As the stock reduction program got underway, the government officials overseeing it were particularly concerned with reducing the number of horses on the reservation. They thought that what little grass there was should be reserved for sheep. Every household on the reservation had to apply for a grazing permit and were allowed only a certain number of horses.

In 1945, Annie was at the district office watching over the permit process. An elderly Navajo grandmother had a palomino horse with a colt. For some reason, she had not received a grazing permit for the horse and had come to see the district supervisor to get permission to keep the horse. Few people had cars or pickups in those days, and the grandmother explained that she used the horse to go to the trading post to buy flour. She also used it to help drag in wood for her cooking and heating fires. But the supervisor was not sympathetic and threw the horse into the corral to be auctioned off.

Annie was very disturbed by the unfairness of the supervisor's actions. She stepped into the corral, grabbed a rope, and lassoed the horse. As she began pulling the horse out of the corral, the supervisor came and grabbed the rope. Annie hung on while the old grandmother stood between them, pleading for her horse.

With quick thinking, Annie jerked the rope out of the supervisor's hands and whipped the horse on its flanks. After all this commotion, the horse took off running, probably for its home corral. Annie told the official that if he wanted the horse, he'd have to go get it.

The supervisor was outraged, of course, but Annie told him, "Let her have the horse as long as she lives. She's not going to last too long."

In fact, the woman ended up living another 30 years and didn't die until she was well over 100 years old. A few years after the event at the corral, Annie arranged for the old woman to get a permit to keep the horse and a couple dozen sheep.

"That was my first battle," Annie recalled.

Navajo Tribal Chairman, Henry Chee Dodge, served from 1922-1928 and 1942-1946. Photo taken May 19, 1946.
  (Photographed by Milton Snow, Courtesy of the Navajo Nation Museum, Window Rock, AZ, Catalog No. NO9-51.)

It seemed that the older Chee Dodge became in years, the more modern were his ideas. He felt strongly that it was important for the Navajos to learn new ways to ensure their survival as a people. He continued to push for increased education for Navajos and thought boarding schools were a good idea, since by spending day and night at the schools the students were immersed in modern ways. He thought all Navajos should learn English so they could compete for jobs. He also lobbied for full citizenship and the right to vote in state and federal elections for all Indians in Arizona and New Mexico.

Chee was in poor health after a heart attack, but in 1946 he decided to run for tribal chairman again. He came in second, so he was going to be vice chairman.

But Chee never took office. Around Thanksgiving he entered Sage Memorial Hospital in Ganado. Annie, George, and Chee's other children along with their spouses came to his bedside every day.

At last, Chee had a talk with his doctor and learned that the end was near. He called all of his children to circle his bedside. Chee Dodge was always an eloquent speaker and his talk to his children on his deathbed was no exception. He gave them advice for how to carry on his legacy of working for the Navajos. He told them, "Do not let my straight rope fall to the ground. If you discover it dropping, quickly one of you pick it up and hold it aloft and straight." He was using a metaphor to urge them to carry on his lifetime of work for the Navajo people. He may have been comparing the leading of the Navajos to the training of a horse. When someone is working with a horse on a long training rope, it is necessary to keep the rope taut and straight to control the animal.

Chee died the next morning on January 7, 1947. Although traditional Navajos at that time did not speak of the dead and conducted burials quickly, Chee had a big funeral at St. Michaels mission with many tributes.

When Chee's property was divided, it was decided that Mary and her husband Carl Peshlaki would manage the ranch at Sonsola Buttes, Ben and his family would take another section of it, and Annie and George would remain at Tanner Springs. Annie's oldest brother Tom had already served the Navajos as chairman for one session and had left the reservation.

During the four years between Chee's death and the next election, Annie began to think about running for a seat on the Navajo Tribal Council, representing Wide Ruins and Klagetoh. She talked to people in her district. The women all urged her to run and some men were also supportive. As expected, the older, more traditional men thought her job as a wife and mother should come first, and they counseled her to stay home at the ranch.

But in a way, Annie's entire life had prepared her for this moment. She had been surrounded by politics as a child growing up in Chee's busy household. Now 41 years old, she had attended chapter meetings and acted as a translator when necessary, served on the grazing committee, and been elected chapter secretary.

The fact that the tribal councils had always been all men was not entirely the doing of the Navajos themselves. Women have traditionally held leadership roles in the family and chapters. But the first Navajo tribal boards had been established by white men in the days when women were not allowed to vote. During the previous election, a woman from another district had been the first woman to be elected to the Navajo Tribal Council. This woman, Lily J. Neil, had been very active in her role, but after a bad car accident, she had decided not to run for re-election.

After a great deal of thought and talking it over with her

Navajo Tribal Council Chambers in Window Rock, Arizona.
(Photographed by Milton Snow, Courtesy of the Navajo Nation Museum, Window Rock, AZ, Catalog No. NO11-269.)

Navajo Council Delegates, Window Rock, Arizona. Photo taken in 1951.
(Photographed by Milton Snow, Courtesy of the Navajo Nation Museum, Window Rock, AZ, Catalog No. NO11-693.)

husband George, Annie decided to run for a council seat.

The election was held on May 5 and 6, 1951. The secret ballots each had a photo of the candidate beside his or her name so that voters who could not read knew where to mark their X. People came from all corners of the reservation to vote, arriving by wagon, horseback, and truck. When the votes were counted, Annie had won the right to represent Wide Ruins and Klagetoh chapters in Window Rock (*Tségháhoodzání*, "perforated rock"), the capital of the Navajo Nation. Two of Annie's brothers also won seats. Ben would represent Crystal (*Tó Niłts'ílí*, "clear water"), New Mexico and Justin Shirley, Keehanabah's son, would represent Sawmill, Arizona.

When Annie started her career as a delegate to the Navajo Tribal Council, she began what would be a lifetime of work. Most people, when first elected to the Tribal Council, sat back and listened for the first few weeks or months, observing how the more experienced council members operated. But Annie didn't start her new job slowly. In fact, in her very first session as a delegate, she stood up to speak. She was concerned to see the white Bureau of Indian Affairs administrator sitting in the front of the Tribal Council. He sat right next to the chairman, Sam Ahkeah, and kept whispering in his ear what to do. Annie thought this behavior made it appear that the Navajos were being controlled by the BIA. She stood up and made a long speech condemning what she saw, and from then on, the superintendent did not sit in the front. She was also concerned that too many tribal positions were going to white people when she thought that Navajos could do those jobs just as well.

On most of the days that the council was in session, Annie drove back and forth to the ranch at Tanner Springs in the family pickup, a round trip of 150 miles. Because the Navajo Reservation is so large, and the roads were so bad at that time, many of the council delegates stayed overnight in Window Rock. There was a block of small rooms reserved for delegates who lived far from Window Rock. If the weather was bad or the session had run late, Annie would spend the night there.

Fortunately, George was willing to take on more duties at the ranch and watch over the children. There were also hired hands and Shirley, one of Keehanabah's daughters and half-sister to Annie, who helped out as well.

About a year after Annie took her council seat, the Tribal Council decided to send a delegation to Washington, DC, to lobby the federal government. Annie was chosen to go along with a group of male delegates. It was thought that the men would behave better if Annie were on the trip. So on a cold February morning, long before the sun was up, Annie and the others boarded the Santa Fe Chief at the train station in Gallup for the long trip to Washington. We can only imagine how excited she must have been to start the long trip across the United States to the nation's capital. Until that time, except for school in Albuquerque, she had rarely been off the reservation, and she had never been outside of Arizona (*Béégashii Nit'ání*, "where the cows grow up") and New Mexico (*Yootó Bináhásdzo*, "get"). Now she was headed to Washington, DC, to talk to the most powerful leaders in the country.

Annie Wauneka in Washington.
(Courtesy National Archives, photo no. 75-TLA-19-PO-1-D.)

Chapter 4

One morning Annie walked into the council chambers in Window Rock, and as she was taking her seat, she saw that two doctors had come to address the Tribal Council. The doctors told the delegates that an epidemic of tuberculosis on the reservation had reached an extreme point. All the beds for tuberculosis patients at the hospital in Fort Defiance were filled, and Navajo patients were going to have to be sent to hospitals in other communities in the Southwest.

These doctors and others were to return to the council many times to discuss the growing problem of tuberculosis, called TB for short. At one point they did have some good news. A new drug had been discovered that could help cure tuberculosis, but the cure was not instant. It had to be taken over a period of time. The bad news was that sick Navajos were not coming in for treatment. Those who did come were not staying long enough for the drug to cure them. Tuberculosis can be easily passed from one family member to another, and sanitation was poor in the hogans. The doctors had another message for the Tribal Council members: You must help us to stop this disease.

Annie Waunkea and the Tribal Council.
(Leslie Goodluck Collection, Cline Library, Northern Arizona University. Catalog No. NAU.PH.2003.13.4.4.)

What happened next was to change Annie's life forever. Following is a story she told many times:

"Doctors reported that the tuberculosis was killing Navajos like flies," she said. "This man, a council delegate, he got up and looked around and said, 'Where's the lady?' He said, 'You women can take care of the sick far better than we men can. So let's appoint her and get her to work.' I'd heard about the tuberculosis, but there was nothing I knew about tuberculosis. They didn't even give me a chance to say yes or no. Made a motion, second, voted, and I was in. I had my work cut out."

In this way, Annie became the chairperson of the new Health and Welfare Committee. Her childhood experience of helping to nurse students during the flu epidemic of 1918 was still in the back of her mind. She had not been able to do much to save their lives then. Maybe now she could do more to help save the lives of Navajos who had contracted tuberculosis.

Because Annie was now in charge of leading the Tribal Council work on the tuberculosis issue, she listened closely when a Bureau of Indian Affairs doctor named Kurt Deuschle (pronounced doy-shill) gave the council an update on the fight against the disease. He needed to put the science of the disease into plain words for the delegates, many of whom had a limited education.

Dr. Deuschle explained, "Tuberculosis most commonly affects a person's lungs, but it can also affect his brain and bone, his bowels and his kidneys. We know that this condition is caused by a living, growing organism, which cannot be seen by the naked eye. It is necessary to take an instrument, called a microscope, and examine the sputum or spit of a person. Through the microscope the doctor sees the tubercle – which appears as a small red worm – and it is this organism which causes tuberculosis. I think it is very important to point out that the way tuberculosis is spread is through the cough of a person who has tuberculosis of the

Annie Wauneka at Mexican Hat, UT for a public meeting.
(Courtesy of the Navajo Nation Museum, Window Rock, AZ, Catalog No. L-PRC.)

lung. When he coughs, he sprays out these germs, these little red worms. The healthy person that breathes the air in which this spray is found is subject to tuberculosis. As many as ten others can get tuberculosis from that one person."

After Dr. Deuschle told the delegates how people got TB, he told them about the treatment with the new medicine. Patients needed bed rest and good food for the medicine to work properly. They also needed to stay in the hospital until they were cured. Staying in the hospital was the main problem. The TB patients, both those sent to hospitals off the reservation and those at the hospital in Fort Defiance, were leaving before they were totally cured. As soon as they began feeling a little better, they would write a letter to their relatives and a pickup truck would arrive and take the sick man or woman home.

Annie learned that leaving the hospital early was a problem for two reasons. When a person was still sick, they could still infect others. And a person who was not totally cured would get sick again and either die or have to go back to the hospital.

Dr. Deuschle also explained how the drugs worked. At first, the drug kills off the weakest germs. The stronger germs take longer to kill. When a patient stops taking the drug too soon, the stronger germs come back with even more power. Should the sick person decide to come back to the hospital, the drugs will not be as effective the second time.

Finally, Dr. Deuschle threw up his hands in frustration and asked the delegates, "Why are these patients leaving before their treatment is completed and what can we do about it?"

Annie knew it was her job to help him find the answer. The health of her people depended on it. However, Annie didn't think she knew enough about the disease to talk about it to others. So she went to Dr. Deuschle and asked him to teach her about tuberculosis. For three months she studied with him, talked to patients, looked at infected sputum under the microscope, and looked at X-rays of infected lungs on the light box. She learned that tuberculosis is a world-wide disease, affecting people on every continent.

"I wanted to see with my own eyes what kind of bugs the doctors were talking about," she said. "I had to know there actually were germs. To explain to other Navajos about tuberculosis, I had to find out all about it – what it could do to a human being, where it came from."

Maybe someone else given the responsibility of heading the Health and Welfare Committee would have just made a series of reports to the council, telling them what she had learned. But that was not Annie's way. Following the lead of her father Chee Dodge, she made the problem of the sick Navajos her problem.

At last the day came when Annie thought she knew enough about tuberculosis to teach others. Leaving her family in the care of George and other helpers at Tanner Springs, Annie got into her pickup truck and began driving around the Southwest to visit the patients in the hospitals. Her first stop was a hospital in Colorado Springs with more than 400 Navajo patients. The word spread quickly through the hospital that someone from the Tribal Council had come to visit. They were sure Annie had come to take them home. But Annie had quite a different message for them. She told them how important it was for them to stay in the hospital – maybe for another six months, maybe longer. They would need to stay until they were cured.

This news was disappointing to the sick Navajos. Hospitals were such strange places in their eyes. The typical Navajo of that day lived in a snug, dark hogan, slept on sheepskins around the fire surrounded by relatives, and ate mutton and fry bread and occasionally such vegetables as corn. They were very modest, never undressed in front of anyone, and slept in their clothes.

The hospitals were all painted white, and they were anything but cozy. The patients had to wear pajamas, people were always

Annie Wauneka at Gallup Hospital.
(Photo by Carl Iwaski / Time & Life Pictures / Getty Images.)

examining them, and the food was not what they were used to eating. And of course everybody knew many people died in hospitals. The Navajos believed such places of death were full of evil spirits. If you weren't sick when you went in, you'd surely become ill in such a place.

Despite all this, Annie reminded patients that things weren't so bad in the hospital – they got to rest in a clean bed and eat three healthy meals a day.

To help the sick Navajos understand why it was important that they stay in the hospital, Annie explained to them in their own language everything she knew about TB. She took them to the hospital laboratory and showed them their sputum under a microscope. The fluid had been stained so they could see the bright red organisms that were causing their illness. Annie also showed them their X-rays, and interpreted while doctors pointed out the diseased parts of their lungs.

Of course, even when the patients understood why they had to stay in the hospital, they were very lonely for home. To help with this loneliness, Annie carried a tape recorder with her. These weren't the little cassette recorders we have now, but the old-fashioned reel-to-reel type. After lugging this into the hospitals, she would record patients' voices for the folks back home. They could ask how everybody was doing and how the sheep were faring. When Annie returned to the reservation, she was able to tape the voices of the families to send or take to the patients. She always coached the families to be reassuring that all was fine with the livestock and to urge the patient to stay in the hospital until well.

After Colorado, Annie drove to other hospitals where Navajos with tuberculosis were being cared for, staying about a week at each hospital.

Getting the hospitalized Navajos to understand what having tuberculosis meant and convincing them to stay until they were cured was only a part of the battle Annie faced. Doctors working on the Navajo tuberculosis project again came to report their progress to the Tribal Council. They said that it appeared the new drugs were working very well on about half the patients, somewhat on about a fourth of the patients, and not at all on the remaining fourth. Doctors told the delegates that they were very concerned because if a patient who had been taking the new drugs left the hospital before being cured, the patient would pass on a type of tuberculosis that was drug-resistant.

There was another piece of bad news. Although the doctors estimated there were between 1,200 and 1,500 active cases of tuberculosis on the reservation, only a few hundred of the sick people were in hospitals. The others either refused to go to the hospital or left before they were cured. This meant that not only were they in danger of becoming sicker and perhaps dying from their disease, but it also meant that every time they coughed or shared a cup or a spoon, they were spreading it to other family members as well.

What to do about the sick Navajos who refused to go for treatment had been discussed many times in the Tribal Council meetings. In some epidemics in other places, the government has ruled that sick people must be segregated from healthy people, usually in something like a hospital. The sick people have no choice; they must either stay in their homes and be quarantined or go to the special place set up for them. Annie and the other Navajos on the Tribal Council did not want to make a law like this, because they said it would make the hospitals like a prison. They hoped that by educating the Navajos, the sick would understand the importance of getting treatment and go to the doctor voluntarily.

Annie continued to believe that she could talk people into

The Waunekas visit the Yazzies.
(Photo by Carl Iwaski / Time & Life Pictures / Getty Images.)

going to the hospital for treatment or testing. That way, the people would get better themselves and spare their family members from contracting their illness. She set out to find these people who were suspected of carrying TB. She knew she would have to use all of her skills of compromise and humor to get through to them.

Sometimes Annie traveled with nurses or other health officials. Frequently she went alone. In those days, members of the Navajo Tribal Council always wore a badge that identified them to others. Since Navajos are very fond of nicknames, Annie became known as "The Woman with the Badge."

Annie's travels around the large reservation were not easy. There were less than 200 miles of paved roads. Sometimes Annie steered her pickup truck along tracks visible only because someone's wagon had passed by often enough to crush the grass. Frequently the tracks were rocky and she had to drive very slowly to ease her truck over the bumps. She always carried a shovel in the back of the truck and knew how to dig herself out when she got stuck.

Sometimes Annie found herself too far from Window Rock or Tanner Springs to return home in the evening. On those days, she stayed with whichever family she had been visiting at the end of the day. The Navajo families were honored to have an important visitor and were generous even if their evening meal was nothing but fry bread and tea. Despite her more privileged life, Annie was content to lie down on a sheepskin next to the stove with the family she was visiting. The next morning she would be on her way again.

One problem was that the homes she was visiting usually had a member with an active case of tuberculosis. Annie had to be careful not to offend her hosts while protecting her own health. She always directed that the water she was to drink and the cup she would use had to be boiled to kill any germs. She hoped that the people she was visiting would learn from her example.

Many of the sick Navajos that Annie visited knew they had an illness and had consulted their nearest medicine man, hoping he could cure them. These wise old men were part doctor, part herbalist, and part psychologist. Unfortunately, tuberculosis was too strong a disease and could not be cured with even the bitterest herb. A sick person might spend valuable time finding just the right medicine man, then in planning a ceremony, then waiting for the ceremony to work. This process could take months. Meanwhile, the disease was getting worse and probably spreading to other family members.

Not all of the people with tuberculosis were adults. Many were children. One of those children was Albert Hale, who would grow up to become president of the Navajo Nation in 1995. He might not have even made it out of grade school if it hadn't been for Annie Wauneka. Albert's family lived in Klagetoh, and Annie was related to his family though their clans. "The Woman with the Badge" would occasionally stop to visit the Hale's home and always took the opportunity to talk about tuberculosis and health.

Albert was eight years old when he contracted TB. His parents, who were very traditional, called in a medicine man. Albert was extremely sick, near death, and the medicine man prayed over him, sang sacred songs, and painted his body black. But it didn't help. Albert's mother was holding him and crying because she was afraid she was going to lose him. Finally, the family decided to follow the advice Annie had given so often – to seek the advice of the white doctors. Albert's parents managed to contact someone with a truck, and they drove him to Ganado to Sage Memorial Hospital. There the doctors began to treat him immediately. Albert stayed in the hospital for months, and he remembers that Annie stopped by to visit him there.

After witnessing too many of these situations, Annie knew

she needed to begin educating the medicine men so that they would become partners in combating this terrible disease that was spreading over their land. As long as the medicine men continued to offer hope that their traditional treatments would work, more and more people would get sick. On Annie's long drives through the sagebrush, she pondered this problem over and over. How could she share what she knew about tuberculosis with the medicine men?

Chapter 5

Navajo medicine men are honored for their knowledge of ways to heal both physical and psychological illnesses. They are also feared for their power over supernatural forces. Annie wanted to approach them in a respectful manner, so she and the Bureau of Indian Affairs doctors decided to arrange meetings with the medicine men in the various parts of the reservation.

Annie and the doctors thought the best way to teach the medicine men about the importance of referring patients with tuberculosis to the hospitals would be to give them the same information she had received when she became head of the Health and Welfare Committee. Groups of about a dozen medicine men came in and heard the doctors explain how tuberculosis spread and how it affected the bodies of those infected. The medicine men were able to look at the sputum of a sick person under a microscope and see the "little red worms" for themselves. Many of the native healers were old men and did not speak English, so Annie acted as translator.

A group of Navajo medicine men from the Crownpoint area visit the Fort Defiance Hospital Sanatorium. March 5, 1954.

(Photographed by Milton Snow, Courtesy of the Navajo Nation Museum, Window Rock, AZ, Catalog No. NK10-71.)

The medicine men did not change their beliefs overnight. They had been taught the traditional view, which was that tuberculosis was caused by a lightning strike or a problem with a certain ceremony. It was very difficult for them to accept that a person could become deathly ill just by being near someone who coughed.

One story Annie liked to tell demonstrated how difficult it was in those years to convince the medicine men that the treatment of tuberculosis was better left to doctors using modern medicine. Annie and a public health nurse had been looking for a young woman named Elizabeth who had run away from the hospital where she was being treated. They found her at a cattle sale being held at a trading post near Rock Point (*Tsé Ntsaa Deez'áhí*, "big rock point"), Arizona.

Annie was talking to Elizabeth near a corral when the young woman's grandfather, a well-known medicine man, came up and blamed Annie for taking his daughter away and making her sick. Annie tried to explain that she was trying to save Elizabeth, but the medicine man was convinced somebody was paying Annie to take people away to die. Annie had a very forceful way of talking, and apparently the medicine man did too. Soon they were surrounded by other people who had come to the cattle sale. Everybody was supporting the medicine man, clapping every time he ridiculed Annie's explanations.

In those days it was considered very brave, even foolish, to challenge such a powerful medicine man, but Annie knew the battle against tuberculosis had to be fought in just such situations.

"I know how to treat tuberculosis," the medicine man boasted.

"Wonderful," Annie replied. "I've been looking for a Navajo who knows how to cure tuberculosis. Where have you been hiding? I wish you would have come a long time ago. How do you treat tuberculosis?"

The medicine man said that he mixed pinyon pine pitch with grease and sagebrush and boiled it with water. The sick person bathed in the mixture, then took a sweat bath. The patient also swallowed warm pinyon pitch mixed with water.

Then it was Annie's turn to talk about how the white doctors treated tuberculosis. "They get good food, good beds, clean linen. Let 'em sleep an' rest. How about you?" she asked.

"They don't have to do that," the medicine man said.

At that point, Annie realized that it wasn't working to challenge the medicine man directly, so she decided to jolly him along to see where the conversation would go. If he thought his treatment was better than that of the government doctors, she'd see if he was willing to prove it.

"Are you ready to go up against the competition?" Annie asked the old medicine man.

He said he was. So Annie told him that he needed to get all of his medicine ready. He would need to get big bottles of pinyon gum, and it would all need to be sterilized. He would have to build a couple dozen clean, new sweat lodges, sterilize his equipment, bring in some healthy food, and a woman to cook for his patients. In ten days Annie would come back and take him to Fort Defiance, where he would compete with the white doctors with their needles full of medicine and their operating rooms.

The crowd was continuing to clap and cheer. Then two older women came out of the crowd. These women apparently had gained courage from Annie and were willing to speak against the medicine man. They accused him of drinking too much.

Shortly after that, the medicine man came up to Annie and said he had decided he would not continue to treat tuberculosis. Annie asked him to tell his granddaughter to go back to the hospital. The next day Annie and the nurse picked up Elizabeth and returned her to the Fort Defiance tuberculosis ward. Elizabeth recovered and lived a long life. Whenever she saw Annie, she came up to greet her.

Although progress was slow, the medicine men and the white doctors did begin working together. The government doctors agreed that if a person were not so ill that they needed to be in the hospital right away, they could wait a short time before they went in. During this time they could locate a medicine man who could perform the right traditional ceremony or sing so they could be protected and blessed.

Some doctors allowed the medicine men to enter the operating rooms to offer a blessing before the rooms were sterilized for surgery. There was even a discussion about a hogan being built outside of the Tuba City Hospital so that Navajo children already hospitalized would be able to have a sing without having to travel. Each of these important steps required lots of talk so that both sides felt their views were respected and their concerns were being heard. Annie was in the midst of all of these negotiations: translating, moving from one group to the other, helping each side to understand the other side and give up some of their own demands.

As the medicine men received more respect from the government doctors and felt they were being treated as colleagues and partners, they began to refer more of their tuberculosis patients to the hospitals.

Once the patients were hospitalized, visits from the medicine men, the patients' families, Annie, and other members of the Health and Welfare Committee were very helpful to the sick Navajos. It was important to help the patients exchange letters with their relatives back home. Medical reports said these visits were as important in treating the homesickness as the new drugs were in treating tuberculosis. In some ways, treating the homesickness was the most important treatment, because patients who were

Gallup Ceremonial exhibits on tuberculosis. August 1954.
(Photographed by Milton Snow, Courtesy of the Navajo Nation Museum, Window Rock, AZ, Catalog No. NK10-89.)

too lonely simply left the hospital and went back to their hogans before the drugs had a chance to work.

But there was still the problem of getting sick Navajos to visit the doctor in the first place and of convincing them to accept treatment. The Navajo Reservation is huge with many remote canyons, mesas, and sheep camps. It would take more than just a few people to tell everybody about the new treatments. Annie worked with the government doctors, trying many ways to spread the word about tuberculosis. Her message: tuberculosis meant sure death, but if the sick people came to the hospital they could be cured. She put together a special class and invited some of the most important members of the Tribal Council to attend, hoping that when they returned to their chapters they would take the information back to the people who had elected them.

Annie worked with the Bureau of Indian Affairs Health Department to make some movies about tuberculosis and childhood diarrhea, another widespread health problem. Annie talked her friends and relatives into being stars in these movies. The movies were all in the Navajo language, and they were shown wherever there was a place with electricity that people could gather.

The work the Navajos and the government were doing to combat tuberculosis was getting some national attention. A famous reporter named Walter Cronkite came to the reservation and made a television program that featured Annie. She was visiting a Navajo family that included an elderly grandmother who had tuberculosis. The grandmother showed Annie a jar of dried herbs that a medicine man had given her to make a bitter tea that she believed would cure her. In the program, Annie tells the old woman to take the pills the doctor had given her along with the tea. "You kind of have to work with them," she told the reporter.

Annie Wauneka at Window Rock.
(Leslie Goodluck Collection, Cline Library, Northern Arizona University. Catalog No. NAU.PH.2003.13.4.5.)

After four years of hard work trying to combat tuberculosis, Annie ran for re-election to the Tribal Council and won easily. However, there was a new tribal chairman, and it was up to him to appoint the chairmen of the various council committees. Annie had been quite visible in her health care work, chairing meetings and giving speeches. As is often the case in many cultures, Navajos tend to distrust people who stand out too far from others. Also, Annie was in an unusual position for a woman. Because of that, there was talk among some of the council members that someone else should be made chairperson of the Health and Welfare Committee.

But Annie stood up in a council session and said she had tried to get some of the other committee members more involved. One member had said he was only interested in rodeos, not health care. Another member said it was too complicated for him, and he didn't understand all the details. Paul Jones, the new tribal chairman, listened to what everyone had to say and decided, wisely, to re-appoint Annie to chair the Health and Welfare Committee.

About this time, Annie and the Tribal Council received an important boost in their fight against tuberculosis. The U.S. Public Health Service replaced the Bureau of Indian Affairs Health Department as a provider of health care to the Navajos. This change meant that there was more money and more attention for health care.

One of the first moves under the Public Health Service was to start a clinic to study whether people with early cases of tuberculosis could be treated at home. There would be an X-ray machine in this clinic so Navajos who came in could be diagnosed. If being treated for tuberculosis didn't always mean living in a hospital for many months, maybe more people would be willing to be helped.

The clinic would also handle other kinds of sickness and perform other procedures, from treating colds to setting broken bones. Today, with easy access to clinics everywhere, it may be difficult to imagine how far Navajos had to travel in those days to receive even basic medical care.

The Tribal Council decided to put the clinic in Many Farms (*Dá'ák'eh Haláni*, "many fields"), Arizona, just beyond Canyon de Chelly (*Tséyi' Etso*, "big canyon"), because it was a typical Navajo community and there was a good road leading to it.

Just as important as having a clinic was having Navajos trained in different kinds of health care jobs so they could help their people. When Annie gave her speech at the opening of the new clinic, she promised that as many jobs as possible would be given to Navajos. That meant they had to be trained. The school for practical nurses was enlarged so that twice as many young women could study there. Both men and women were trained for a new job called "health visitors." Because the public health nurses had so much territory to cover, the health visitors helped by checking the families in their own neighborhoods for illness.

The U.S. Public Health Service sent a very good doctor named James Shaw to lead the office in Window Rock. Dr. Shaw took a broad look at all the health care problems of the Navajos and was surprised to find that most Navajo illnesses were serious infections. Dr. Shaw came to speak to the Tribal Council and said that these illnesses were preventable. "We should be working to keep people well rather than spending so much energy to cure them once they are ill," he said.

For Annie, this was a new challenge. The Woman with the Badge headed out again to drive the back roads and tracks of the reservation. She wasn't exactly sure what she was going to do, but she knew she'd figure it out as she drove.

Chapter 6

Because Annie had had the benefit of a good education at the Albuquerque Indian School, she knew about infections and germs. She knew that having a clean house and body were the keys to keeping people free of infections and other illnesses. She decided she would do what she could to teach her fellow Navajos how to have a tidier and healthier home.

Anytime Annie passed a grocer in town or a trader out on the reservation, she stopped to see if they had any empty boxes or crates. In those days, many of the fruits and vegetables came in wooden crates, and she piled these in the back of her pickup truck. She also collected big, empty lard cans and coffee tins with lids. She washed them until they were clean. When she stopped to visit a hogan and found that the dishes, flour, and sugar were being stored on a dirt floor, she brought in the boxes and stacked them to make a kitchen area. She taught the women to store food in the cans so it would be protected from dirt and insects. When she found a house that had no soap, she took the people a bar and showed them how to use it to wash their hands. Annie also taught the women to heat water and use hot water with soap to wash their dishes, as well as to cover the dishes with a clean towel to keep flies away.

Many Navajos were receiving staple foods from a government surplus commodity program. These foods included flour and cornmeal, which the people knew how to use. There were also some unfamiliar foods like canned minced ham, cheese, and powdered milk. In order to teach the women how to prepare these foods, Annie set up some local education programs.

Because practically everyone she visited had to haul their water and store it in barrels, Annie talked to them about how important it was to get water from a clean source, not a pond or stock tank. When Annie went to a public gathering like a sing or a rodeo, she always asked where the drinking water came from. If it came from a pond, she made them throw it out and get a clean supply from a windmill or a pump.

She also inspected how the food was being prepared. She directed the people running the concessions to clean their utensils and to serve the food with paper plates and cups.

"You are feeding people, not dogs!" Annie told the organizers. Because doing things Annie's way took more time and was more expensive, some people didn't like her telling them how to run their business. But Annie stood up to their criticism.

In her travels to remote households, Annie was shocked to find that many of the children who were not in school were infected with head lice or had bad cases of impetigo, a skin disease. She taught the parents how to treat their children. She also learned that many of the camps had no outhouses, resulting in problems with flies spreading germs and disease. The Public Health Service had begun training Navajos as sanitation technicians, and Annie directed these workers to teach people how to build proper outhouses.

Annie had to handle these visits with much traditional courtesy. In the Navajo way, she would drive up to a hogan, park her pickup truck, and wait until first the dogs and then the people came out to invite her in. She would begin by greeting

Annie Wauneka at the Navajo Tribal Fair in Window Rock, Arizona. Photo taken September 1959.

(Courtesy of the Navajo Nation Museum, Window Rock, AZ, Catalog No. L-566.a.)

everyone and introducing herself, telling them the clan of both her father and mother. She paid particular attention to any elderly family members. She would inquire after everyone's health and relatives and discuss the weather. Only then would she get to the real reason for her visit.

Many traditional Navajos don't believe in telling other people what to do and how to run their lives, so Annie had to be careful in the way she said things. We can only imagine how a Navajo woman might have felt to have a famous person drive up to her home, and sometime during the visit bring in boxes and cans to start rearranging her food and pots and pans. But Annie knew just how to do this without offending too many people.

Annie visited as many people as she could and spoke in chapter houses, but the Navajo Reservation was much too big for her to visit everyone. Then an opportunity came for her to teach many more people how to live a healthier life. She began a weekly radio program broadcast from KGAK, a radio station in Gallup. Even if Navajo families didn't have electricity, they would have a battery-operated radio. Every week Annie would go into the station and record her program in the Navajo language, and it would be broadcast Sunday mornings. In the summer, Annie would talk about problems such as protecting food from flies and treating children who had diarrhea. In the winter, she would talk about pneumonia and colds and protecting babies from cold weather.

Annie's programs were sponsored by Pet Milk. Since most families had no refrigerators, canned evaporated milk was a way that mothers could give their children the milk that would help them build strong bones. People who remember Annie's broadcasts say she always advised breastfeeding rather than bottle feeding, if that were possible.

So many people heard Annie's health programs on the radio

that The Woman with the Badge received a second nickname: The Milk Lady.

As a mother of many children herself, Annie was able to think of ways to encourage other Navajo mothers to pay closer attention to the health of their children. She encouraged the Navajo Tribal Council to buy simple layettes for newborn babies. If a mother delivered her baby in a hospital or brought the baby into a hospital for a checkup within two weeks of being born, she would receive a layette with a few soft blankets and some baby clothes.

Annie also started a baby contest at the annual Navajo Tribal Fair. Adorable Navajo babies and toddlers with their shiny brown hair and dark eyes were judged not only on their cuteness, but also on their health. Doctors were able to examine the many babies that were entered into the contest. If any health problems were found, the mothers could be offered advice or referred to a clinic.

As Annie traveled to the remote hogans, she saw that many of the Navajos she visited would find it impossible to follow the advice she gave them for living a more healthful life. Their hogans had dirt floors and the doors and windows were covered only with a blanket in cold weather. In warm weather, the doors and windows had no coverings. The corrals for the sheep and horses were near the hogans, so in the summer flies were a problem. The flies would visit the corrals, crawl on the manure, and then fly into the hogans and dirty the food and dishes. The flies would crawl around the mouths and eyes of the babies, giving them infections.

Navajos who had been cured of tuberculosis and children who had recovered from infections went back to these difficult living conditions and got re-infected. Annie knew that these people needed to improve their homes with wooden floors, solid

Annie Wauneka and Miss Navajo.
(Leslie Goodluck Collection, Cline Library, Northern Arizona University. Catalog No. NAU.PH.2003.13.4.3.)

doors, and glass and screens on the windows. But she also knew that for many of these families, finding the money for these improvements would be impossible. The money would have to come from elsewhere.

Annie and the other members of the Health and Welfare Committee went to the Tribal Council and asked for an appropriation of money to help the poorest Navajos improve their homes. "Housing is so critical on the reservation, we don't have housewives, we have shack wives!" Annie told anyone who would listen.

The other council members didn't see the need for the improvements and they voted down the committee's request. Annie was furious. And when Annie decided something needed to be done, she found a way to make it happen.

For three months, Annie talked to people about the housing problem whenever she happened to be on the reservation. She talked to people who had relatives in the hospital. She told them that if they didn't want their loved ones to come back to a bad living situation, they should ask their council representative to vote for the program. Council members who had relatives who had been cured or were currently in the hospital got a visit from Annie.

"Do you want your loved ones to come back to an unhealthy home and get sick again?" Annie asked them.

Annie thought it was only fair that the funds be spent to help the poorest people. Much of the tribal budget was money that belonged to all the Navajo people, as it came from the oil and gas leases the Tribal Council granted to energy companies. Annie's months of work paid off. When the council met again, they voted $300,000 for a better housing program and the federal government contributed some money as well.

"I threatened them," Annie explained later with her booming laugh that shook her whole body. "It worked!"

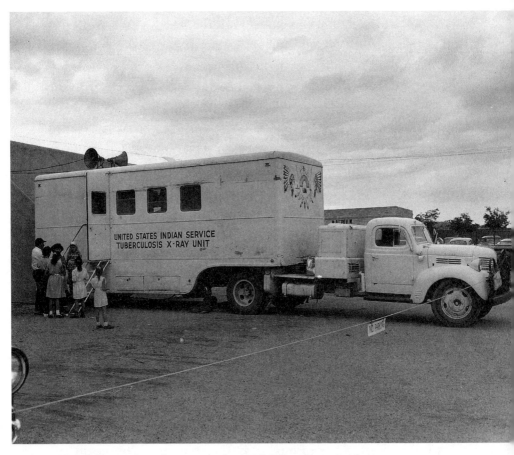

Mobile X-ray tuberculosis unit at the 1954 Gallup Ceremonial.
(Photographed by Milton Snow, Courtesy of the Navajo Nation Museum, Window Rock, AZ, Catalog No. NK10-97.)

This was not the only time Annie had to think of a ploy to get the other members of the Tribal Council to support her. One summer, the Public Health Service had a new mobile X-ray truck that was going to head out to the reservation to check people for tuberculosis. Annie arranged for the truck to come first to the council headquarters in Window Rock so that all the council delegates and the people who worked for the council could be checked. She wanted the delegates to be able to go back to their chapters and explain the program to their neighbors, but she also suspected that several of them had undiagnosed TB. If that were correct, she wanted them to start treatment.

By January 1959, Annie had been working for seven years to try to combat tuberculosis and improve the health of the Navajos. New drugs were helping patients to recover, leave the hospitals, and go back to their lives. Other people with early cases of tuberculosis were being treated as outpatients at the new clinic in Many Farms. They, too, were getting well.

But the rate of tuberculosis was still five or six times higher on the reservation than in the surrounding states. This was because nearly half the Navajos infected with tuberculosis were still refusing treatment. Those infected would give the excuse that they needed time to arrange a traditional ceremony before they left for the hospital, or they needed to move their sheep to summer pasture, or they had to get a corral repaired. But time would pass, and still they would not go for treatment. And as long as they stayed in their homes, they were getting sicker and passing the disease to their families and friends.

When she first began her fight against TB, Annie had thought that if she could spread the word about the new treatments, and if she could make the conditions in the hospitals more pleasant, then people would agree to be treated. Week after week she had driven on lonely roads to far-off hogans, she had given speeches in the chapter houses, and she had talked individually to people she knew were infected. Yet some of them still refused treatment. What else could the Tribal Council do?

The Navajo Reservation spreads over three states, Arizona, New Mexico, and Utah. Each of these states had laws that said people with active cases of tuberculosis could be sent to a hospital and made to stay there until they were no longer contagious. But the Navajo Reservation was a special situation, and it was up to the Surgeon General of the United States to decide whether Navajo patients could be forced to go to the hospital. The Surgeon General would do this only on the request of the Tribal Council.

Annie and several government doctors went before the Tribal Council to present the situation. Of course, the council delegates hated the idea of having their neighbors hauled into court and then made to stay in the hospital against their will. This idea went against the traditional Navajo way of trying not to tell others how to live their lives. For two days the council discussed the problem. Annie, too, did not like the idea of legally forcing people to get treatment, but she knew no other way. She also reminded the delegates that she had been to Washington, DC, several times asking the federal government for money to fight TB. She warned that if they as a tribe weren't active in the program, they could expect the money to be cut off.

Finally, on the third day of discussion, the vice chairman of the council, a medicine man himself, got up to speak.

"I have a grandchild, a woman, who I tried to convince to go to a hospital. She objected. Finally I convinced her and she said she would go in four days. Before the four days were up, she had a hemorrhage and died. While I made every effort to have her go to the hospital within the last hours, it was too late."

When the vote came, most of the delegates agreed they should ask the health service to request that the Surgeon General put into place the regulation called "involuntary commitment." Navajos infected with tuberculosis would have to go into the hospital for treatment whether they wanted to or not.

Annie had won one more battle. But there were others that lay ahead, health battles that would be much more difficult for her to win.

Chapter 7

T he arrival of the Public Health Service on the Navajo Reservation meant more hospitals and more white government doctors. These arrivals were good news for the Navajos, but it meant problems for Navajo patients who didn't speak English. While there were also more Navajo nurses and health aides, they weren't always available when doctors needed a translator. To help, Annie and some of the medical people had been working for two years on a Navajo-English medical dictionary. The dictionary was valuable for two reasons: to find out what was bothering the patients and later to tell the sick people how they would be treated.

Compiling the dictionary wasn't an easy task. Many of the diseases and conditions had no names in Navajo. Also, because of the way the Navajo language is constructed, it was not possible to simply substitute a Navajo word for an English word. Instead, whole ideas needed to be translated. Even Navajo speakers needed help to explain the sometimes complicated medical situations.

One of the doctors told a story showing why careful translation was so important. On this particular day, a trained medical translator was not available when he was needed to explain something to a patient. The doctor looked around and the only Navajo he could locate quickly was the janitor. The doctor was trying to tell the patient he needed to do surgery on a thyroid tumor, located in the neck. After the janitor translated for the doctor, the patient got up off the chair and ran out of the office in terror. It took the doctor a while to find out the problem. It turns out that instead of fully explaining the surgery, the interpreter had simply told the sick man that the doctor intended to cut his throat!

When Annie and the doctors completed the work on the medical dictionary, it was a great help to the medical personnel, the translators, and of course the sick people themselves.

As Annie became more active in Indian health issues, she traveled to conferences in Arizona, New Mexico, Washington, DC, and other states. Sometimes she sat in the audience and learned from medical speakers. Sometimes she was the expert who gave the speech. People off the reservation began to recognize how much work she was doing for her people, and they gave her awards. In 1959 she received the Indian Council Fire Achievement Award from a group of Indians representing many tribes. Her father Chee Dodge had received the same award in 1945, and this was the first time it had gone to both a parent and child. In that same year, Annie was given the Josephine B. Hughes Memorial Award, an award in honor of an early Arizona governor's wife. Annie was also named Arizona Woman of the Year by the Arizona Press Women's Club. No Indian had ever received these awards before.

Annie Wauneka at the Education Center in Window Rock, Arizona.
(Photo by Kenji Kawano. Courtesy of the photographer.)

In the early 1960s, the Navajo Tribal Council accepted the fact that another terrible disease was affecting their people – the disease of alcoholism – and they decided to take steps to deal with it. Since Annie had shown so much talent in leading the fight against tuberculosis, she was the natural choice to lead the new Alcoholism Committee. Alcoholism was a problem dear to her heart because several people in her own family had problems with alcohol.

As she did when facing her first health care fight, Annie first went to all the doctors and tried to study the problem. Why were so many Navajos ruining their lives by drinking too much wine or other liquor? The Alcoholism Committee hired an expert to help them put together a report. The consultant interviewed many Navajos, read the research, and talked to the doctors, but he found there were no easy answers to the problem of alcoholism on the reservation. Even though the sale of alcohol was illegal on the reservation, 70 percent of adults drank and 80 percent of young people between the ages of 17 and 24 drank, although not all of them were alcoholics. They purchased liquor in Gallup or bought it from bootleggers on the reservation. Most of the Navajos were drinking fortified wine, a drink that was cheaper than other drinks, but more dangerous for their bodies.

The report said that the main reason for the heavy drinking was despair. Many of the men were unemployed. There were few jobs on the reservation, and people didn't want to leave home to find a job. Also, many of them had four years or less of school, which was not enough to find a skilled job.

Annie finished the report to the Tribal Council by saying that the people she talked to wanted help.

"It is just that they cannot overcome this habit," she said. "Once they start drinking they just lose themselves. They seem to think that matters are hopeless, and it is very encouraging to people when someone takes an interest in carrying out a

Annie Wauneka at the well.
  (Photo by Carl Iwaski / Time & Life Pictures / Getty Images.)

rehabilitation program for them."

At the time, the chairman of the Navajo Tribe was Raymond Nakai. He and Annie disagreed on many aspects of caring for the Navajo people. So, although Annie had become known throughout the United States as an expert in Indian health care, Raymond Nakai did not appoint her to the Health Committee.

This situation made Annie's job a little more difficult, but she wasn't going to let a little thing like her committee assignment stop her work.

One of the issues she worked on was rural water systems. At that time the Southwest, and particularly the Navajo Reservation, was facing a severe drought and families were finding it difficult to get clean water. Drinking dirty water causes sickness, and the deaths on the reservation from diseases of the stomach and intestines were twenty times higher than they were in other parts of the country.

The health aides could tell the people to use clean water, but if the only source within miles was a scummy pond, then people didn't have much choice. Fortunately, on the basis of lobbying by Annie and others, the government in Washington voted for funding to drill some wells, put in some water tanks and pipes, and build some sewer systems on the reservation. The hogans were too far apart to provide every household with its own spigot, but Annie worked with the officials to locate the water sources in areas where homes were a little closer to each other. She also made sure the residents knew how to use the new systems.

Being a Tribal Council member was considered only a part-time job. But as Annie became more involved with tribal politics, she was working all day, every day. As Annie had become busier, she had placed some of her older children in the boarding school at St. Michaels. Her other children were still at home. She was lucky that her husband George preferred staying at the ranch and watching over the children, the sheep, and the cattle. He didn't like the hustle and bustle of the towns. He had taken one trip with Annie to Chicago, but he missed his children and his sheep and the wide-open spaces of the ranch. He ended up taking the train home early, leaving the big city behind to return to everything he loved at Tanner Springs. Everyone recognized that it was fortunate for both Annie and the tribe that George was willing to play "Mr. Mom" long before that role was widely accepted for men.

On a hot July day in 1963, Annie received a telegram from Washington, DC, that was to change her life in a big way. The telegram read: "I am happy to inform you of my intention to award you the Presidential Medal of Freedom. This is the highest civil honor conferred by the President of the United States for service in peacetime." The telegram invited her to the White House for the ceremony in September and was signed John F. Kennedy. Annie learned that she had been nominated by Secretary of the Interior Stewart Udall, who had grown up in northern Arizona and knew of her work.

Annie sent a telegram back, accepting and saying in part, "It is with deep humility and gratefulness that this great honor has come to me... I am deeply appreciative of the recognition you have bestowed on me. Your humble servant, Mrs. Annie D. Wauneka."

September was only two months away, so Annie began her preparations. President Kennedy had two young children, so she bought his daughter Caroline a Navajo doll and his little boy John a pair of moccasins. Jacqueline Kennedy, the First Lady, liked to ride horses, so Annie picked out a beautiful, handwoven saddle blanket. She chose a pair of moccasins for the President.

September came and Annie had received no word on the date of the ceremony. She was afraid maybe she had missed the event. She sent a telegram to Washington and got a letter back saying the ceremony was delayed and would probably be in November. By the end of October, she still had received no information. There were few telephones on the reservation then. Again she was worried. Had a message gotten lost? Had she missed the ceremony? She sent another telegram to Washington, and received another answer that President Kennedy had to postpone the ceremony again, this time until December 6.

Then on November 22 the world was shocked to hear that the beloved President John F. Kennedy had been assassinated in Dallas, Texas. President Kennedy was popular with the Navajo people, and they mourned with the rest of the country.

Vice President Lyndon B. Johnson was quickly installed as President. He decided the country needed to get back to work and that the Medal of Freedom ceremony would go on as scheduled. Annie decided she needed more gifts. She bought President Johnson a silver and turquoise bolo tie and for Lady Bird Johnson, the new First Lady, she chose a pin made by a Navajo silversmith. Then she went to Washington, DC.

Annie always wore traditional Navajo dress and the Medal of Freedom ceremony was no exception. When she dressed the morning of the ceremony, she put on a tiered skirt of patterned, dark blue silk that her daughter had sewn for her, and with it she wore a purple velvet blouse with four silver concho pins. Annie also wore some bracelets and silver and turquoise rings. The heavy, silver squash blossom necklace she wore had belonged to Chee Dodge, so it was a way of taking her beloved father along with her on that day.

During the ceremony, each of the Medal of Freedom recipients was called to the front individually. When it was Annie's turn, President Johnson read: "Vigorous crusader for betterment of the health of her people, Mrs. Wauneka has selflessly worked to help them conquer tuberculosis, dysentery and trachoma. She succeeded in these efforts by winning the confidence of her

Annie Wauneka with a doll for Caroline.
(Photo by Carl Iwaski / Time & Life Pictures / Getty Images.)

people, and then by interpreting to them the miracles of modern medical science."

Afterwards, there was a luncheon and a reception. During lunch, she was seated next to the Chief Justice of the Supreme Court, Earl Warren, and was congratulated by many government dignitaries. Secretary of the Interior Stewart Udall introduced her by saying that she was "a one-woman Peace Corps in Navajo land."

It was an amazing experience for Annie, who was once sent to herd sheep while her brothers and sisters were sent to private school, to sit with the President, cabinet members, and Supreme Court justices and receive the highest civilian honor in America.

On December 6, 1963, President Lyndon B. Johnson awarded the Medal of Freedom to Annie Dodge Wauneka.
(LBJ Library Photo by Yoichi Okamoto, W79-5.)

Reception for Annie Wauneka in Secretary Udall's office when she was presented with the Presidential Medal of Freedom, July 1963.
  (Courtesy National Archives, photo no. 75-TLA-19-PO-1-M.)

Chapter 8

After the Medal of Freedom ceremony, Annie headed back to the Navajo Reservation and the many responsibilities that faced her there. She continued to work hard in health care matters. When some cases of bubonic plague erupted on the reservation, she helped doctors send out information through the council delegates and the chapters that children should avoid prairie dogs. The prairie dogs had fleas that were carrying the plague. When the fleas bite people, it causes the plague, which could be deadly if not treated quickly.

Annie also began spending a great deal of her energy on improving education for Navajos. She knew that Navajo children were the future of the tribe, and she was determined that they have an education that would prepare them for the modern world. Traditionally, Navajo children learned what they needed to know about life from their parents and grandparents, but the world was changing too fast. Some of the children's parents didn't speak English or have any education themselves, so that left the schools to guide them.

By now it was the late 1960s, and people all over the country were learning that children who had some time in Head Start before going to school did better and were more prepared to learn to read and write. Children learned how to hold a crayon, how to interact with other children, and how to sit still for a story. Annie worked hard to get Head Start programs on the reservation and to get Navajo parents to do volunteer work in the Head Start programs.

One story shows how committed Annie was to getting Head Start programs on the reservation. By then, she was living in Klagetoh and working with the residents there to get a building for their preschool program. It was winter and some of the men had worked all day putting in forms and preparing for the cement that would be the foundation of the new school. When day's end came, the cement still had not arrived and the men went home. Long after dark a knock came on Annie's door. It was the driver of the cement truck, wondering what to do with his load. Annie knew that to refuse the cement, even at that hour, would mean they would have to pay for it and then order and pay for another load later. She didn't want to waste the funds she had worked so hard for, so she told the driver to wait. She put on her heavy jacket to ward off the cold, and went door to door in Klagetoh, asking the men to come back out to help. Every man she asked agreed to come, and they brought their neighbors as well.

Next, Annie went home and spread a tarp in the back of her pickup truck. She loaded up flour, lard, some large chunks of mutton, and her pots and pans. She also threw in some firewood. Back at the building site she built a fire. While the men moved the cement into the frames for the school foundation, she cooked. It was very late and really cold when they finally finished working. When they came to warm their hands, stiff from the cold, Annie was ready with hot coffee, a bubbling pot of mutton stew, and stacks of fry bread. Annie was not a politician who was content to talk and attend meetings; she was willing to pitch in to get the work done.

Another important matter in education was whether boarding schools or day schools were better for Navajo children. Annie had attended boarding school, and when she was first elected to the Tribal Council, she had supported boarding schools for Navajo children. Annie thought that the children had a healthier living situation at boarding schools, and many children lived too far from a school to travel back and forth every day.

Now, many years later, Annie was changing her mind, particularly when it came to younger children. She had put her own children in boarding school after she was elected to the Tribal Council. Although some of her children did very well at boarding school, others did not. Conditions on the reservation had changed also. Roads were better, so school buses could travel more easily. Living conditions in the hogans had improved, and more people on the reservation had access to good water. Many Navajos began thinking that local schools run by school boards with local chapter residents would be a better way to educate their children. Annie did what she could to help them.

Even attending local schools was difficult for many students because their parents were too poor to buy them decent school clothes. As early as 1954, the Tribal Council had a program to help needy students get school clothing. Sears Roebuck helped by giving discounts.

By the mid-1960s, the Tribal Council was spending more than a million dollars a year to help buy school clothes. But there were problems with the program. The older council members who were making the decisions were not in tune with the current fashions for teenagers. The boys didn't like the pants provided; they wanted only Wrangler jeans, and they didn't like the oxford shoes. Instead, they tore the heels off the oxfords and used them to repair their boots. Annie, as the mother of many children, had more experience with buying clothing for youngsters than the older men on the council did. During one meeting she stood up and talked about the problem.

"Some of us don't like to see the type of clothing our children wear," she said, "but nevertheless, that is the fashion."

There were many situations over the years in which Annie stood up for the Navajo students. Peterson Zah, who eventually became president of the Navajo Nation, remembers a year when he was a student at Phoenix Indian School. The students did not like the food they were being served. As Peterson Zah recalls, it was made from government commodities and it was the same thing day after day with no variety. The students staged a protest against the food. Not knowing how to handle a school full of unhappy students, the school superintendent invited some tribal leaders to come in and resolve the situation.

Annie drove to Phoenix from Klagetoh and met with the administration. She talked to the students and looked at the meals they were being fed. She didn't like what she saw. Some of the representatives from the other tribes were afraid to anger the superintendent, but not Annie. She told him, "We want our children to eat the right food. If they are hungry, you should feed them." She told him she thought it was ridiculous to say that the U.S. government didn't have enough money to feed the children properly.

During these years, Annie was traveling frequently to Washington, DC, and other places in the United States to attend conferences. She learned how to talk to congressmen and other officials, and was eager to share her knowledge with colleagues or younger people who were interested in becoming involved in politics.

She told one young Navajo woman how to approach senators and representatives respectfully. "You don't just go in there

Annie Wauneka with Robert Redford. Annie joined Redford for an ecology conference in 1984.

(Photo by Kenji Kawano. Courtesy of the photographer.)

and say, 'This was our land.' The Eastern senators don't even know that we exist, that there are a people called the Navajo that reside in the Southwest. So you have to introduce yourself and present yourself that you are human too, that you are the first Americans and go about it in a professional manner and a business atmosphere and explain to them fully what you are there for."

Annie always traveled in typical Navajo dress with lots of silver and turquoise jewelry. In airports people would approach her, ask about her clothing, and inquire about the Navajos. Sometimes they were surprised that she spoke English. Annie was always willing to explain to these people that she was a Navajo and tell them about her tribe. Her appearance was helpful when she went to lobby representatives in Congress because she stood out as she walked the halls, going from office to office. Many of the representatives or their assistants knew her and would come out into the hall to greet her.

Walking around Washington, DC, at night when it is dark and the streets are deserted can be dangerous, although it is safer now than it has been in previous years. That didn't stop Annie. If she got bored in her hotel room, she'd go out for a walk. Once when she was cautioned by another traveler to be careful, she opened up her big purse and showed him her protection – a long knife!

Many times Annie's travel took her to conferences where she was given an award for her work. Among them was the Will Ross Medal, the highest award given by the Society of Public Health Educators. She also received an honorary doctorate in humanities from the University of New Mexico in Albuquerque. After that, she usually signed her letters with Dr. Annie Wauneka. This was confusing to children in the schools Annie visited. When they heard that Dr. Wauneka was visiting, they thought she was there to give them a shot. She always reassured them, saying, "I'm just a talking doctor."

All this moving between her simple ranch life and glittery Washington, DC, was not always without a hitch. On one trip, Annie was rushing to get to the airport in Albuquerque. She had to go to the Tanner Springs Ranch and talk to her husband George before she left, and she did some chores while she was there. Then she made a quick stop in Klagetoh to change her clothes before driving to the airport. After the plane had taken off and she had leaned back to relax, she smelled a suspicious barnyard odor. Looking down, she saw her oxfords caked with manure from the corral. She had been rushing so fast that she had forgotten to change her shoes! Annie did her best to hide her feet beneath the seat for the rest of the plane ride.

By the middle of the 1970s, women across the United States were talking about women's liberation. Women wanted the ability to take charge of their own lives, they wanted equal access to opportunities such as education and jobs, and they wanted equal pay for equal work. The Navajo Reservation was no exception to this movement.

Annie Wauneka was appointed to a new Navajo women's commission. Once more, as she had done so many times before, she decided she needed to go out to the reservation to find out what was really going on. She began driving from chapter to chapter, looking into conditions for Navajo women. (As an aside, we should mention that over the years Annie put so many miles on her pickups, driving over bad roads, that she had to go to Gallup and buy a new truck every two years or so.)

Annie called the women to meetings, and together they discussed the problems women faced on the reservation. They talked about their poor housing, the long distances to medical treatment, and what to do if they had relatives who were alcoholics. And they talked about the lack of jobs for themselves on the reservation.

Annie Wauneka with Peterson Zah.
(Photo by Kenji Kawano. Courtesy of the photographer.)

Annie Wauneka with medal.
(Photo by Kenji Kawano. Courtesy of the photographer.)

Sometimes the Navajo men became suspicious of all these meetings. What was Annie up to? So Annie had to meet with the men and explain that it was a new day. She said that women needed a chance to speak up about their problems and work together to solve them.

Annie was the speaker at the first Southwest Indian Women's Conference in the fall of 1973. More than 800 women came from many tribes. Later she talked to the first Navajo Women's Conference. Annie talked to the women about how to blend traditional Indian culture with the white culture. But she warned them not to make it a battle between the sexes. It was important for Native American men and women to be united and to be equal partners.

In 1978, Annie was thinking about not running for re-election, but then decided to run but not to campaign. She ended up losing the election by only 13 votes. For the first time in 26 years, Annie would not be in her seat in the Tribal Council building in Window Rock.

After the shock of her defeat wore off, Annie decided not to retire from public life. She worked to raise money for charities, including the Navajo Nation Health Foundation that was running the hospital in Ganado. She continued to travel to Washington on lobbying trips, and even went to China on a cultural exchange trip.

When Peterson Zah ran for president of the tribe, she traveled with him and gave speeches for him. After he was elected, he appointed her health ambassador for the Navajo people.

On Annie's 74th birthday in 1984, President Zah decided that the Navajo Tribe should honor her for her lifetime of hard work. He scheduled a big birthday party in Window Rock. In both Arizona and New Mexico it was declared "Annie Wauneka Day."

Annie and George Wauneka.
(Photo by Kenji Kawano. Courtesy of the photographer.)

People Annie had worked with over the years came from many states, and school buses brought Navajo children to Window Rock for the festivities. At a ceremony she was called "Our Legendary Mother" and was given a Navajo Medal of Honor. Annie thanked everyone, especially her husband George. All the years Annie had been working so hard for the tribe, George had watched over affairs at the ranch. She had a wonderful career of service, but she knew she couldn't have done it without George's help.

Annie continued working for her beloved Navajos for about eight more years. Then she began to have trouble finding her way around and was confused about some daily activities. Her children, all grown with lives of their own, decided that she needed around-the-clock help and took her to live at the nursing home in Toyei, Arizona. She was diagnosed with Alzheimer's disease and died four years later in October 1997. Albert Hale, whom Annie had helped as a young child with tuberculosis, was then president of the tribe. President Hale closed the tribal government for a day of mourning.

Annie's obituary ran in all the Arizona newspapers and also in the New York Times. The articles mentioned her years of work fighting tuberculosis and alcoholism among the Navajos.

Annie was in some ways a Navajo version of Cinderella. Like Cinderella, as a young child, Annie was made to work while her brothers and sister went to school. But what lifted her up was not a handsome prince, but her own years of hard work and her devotion to her fellow Navajos.

Annie was buried at the Tanner Springs ranch among the junipers and sagebrush in a private family ceremony. The grass grows well there and the lavender mesas guard her memory.

Index

Biography

CAROLYN NIETHAMMER grew up outside Prescott, Arizona. After college, she lived for about six months in rural Northern California and learned from an elderly Indian man how to gather many of the edible wild plants of the area. When she returned to Arizona to live in Tucson, she began to wonder what the native people who lived in the desert had eaten before the white settlers came bringing European crops. Her curiosity led to two years of traveling throughout the Southwest, talking to and cooking with Native American women. Her experiences resulted in her first book, *American Indian Cooking, Recipes from the Southwest*. This book was followed by two others on Native American women, *Daughters of the Earth: The Lives and Legends of Indian Women* and the award-winning biography *I'll Go and Do More: Annie Dodge Wauneka, Navajo Leader and Activist*. This is her eighth book.